REA

FRIEND
OF ACPL

THE HEALING JOURNEY

JOURNEY

for Adult Children of Alcoholics

DARYL E. QUICK

INTERVARSITY PRESS
DOWNERS GROVE, ILLINOIS 60515

InterVarsity Press is the book-publishing division of InterVarsity Christian Fellowship, a student movement active on campus at hundreds of universities, colleges and schools of nursing in the United States of America, and a member movement of the International Fellowship of Evangelical Students. For information about local and regional activities, write Public Relations Dept., InterVarsity Christian Fellowship, 6400 Schroeder Rd., P.O. Box 7895, Madison, WI 53707-7895.

All Scripture quotations, unless otherwise indicated, are from the Holy Bible, New International Version. Copyright © 1973, 1978, International Bible Society. Used by permission of Zondervan Bible Publishers.

ISBN 0-8308-1328-4

Printed in the United States of America

Library of Congress Cataloging-in-Publication Data

Quick, Daryl E.
    The healing journey for adult children of alcoholics/Daryl E.
Quick.
        p.   cm.
    Includes bibliographical references.
    ISBN 0-8308-1328-4
    1. Adult children of alcoholics—Psychology.   2. Adult children of
alcoholics—Rehabilitation.   I. Title.
    HV5132.Q53   1990
    362.29'23—dc20   90-39684
                                                      CIP

13   12   11   10   9   8   7   6   5
99   98

*I have written this book as a fellow traveler on the road to healing.
I, too, grieve the losses of my past and the mistakes I've made on my journey.
I'm thankful for the healing that has taken place. This has helped me to
make better choices for myself and stop the destructive patterns. I look
forward to continual growth so I may live at peace with myself.*

*I want to thank my father for our restored relationship. I want to thank
my mother for her love and tenderness. I am especially indebted to my wife,
Joyce, a fellow ACA, for her support, sacrifices and love.
She has been a key person in restoring my trust in people
and an example of God's promise to heal broken relationships.*

May each of you continue your healing journey.

The Journey Begins

About 35 million people in North America have grown up in alcoholic families. A large majority of these adult children of alcoholics (ACAs) are at high risk for emotional and behavioral problems. While some ACAs are overachievers and super-responsible and appear to have overcome the bad homelife, most will still have difficulty breaking through the rules from childhood and heal the wounds the dysfunctional home created. At a very deep level within the ACA are the rules:

Don't talk.

Don't feel.

Don't trust.

Don't think.

Don't be.

Don't betray the family.

Remain loyal.

Keep the secrets.

The ACA learns to survive by pretending—pretending there is no pain, pretending to know what to do, pretending just to survive the trauma from the home. ACAs become experts at doing, but know little about being at peace within themselves.

Those ACAs who come from religious backgrounds have many of the same difficulties as those who don't. Also, Christians raised in alcoholic homes appeared less liable to experience comfort, God's love and forgiveness; to trust in God's will; to believe in the promises of the Bible and less able to forgive others (Wilson, 1989).

I, too, am an ACA. In my father's family are numerous alcoholics. The early childhood years were very hard for me. I learned to fear his power and inconsistency. I wanted so much to please him, but the target continued to shift. It has taken years for the two of us to grow together in love, respect and forgiveness. He is true evidence of the healing work of God. For the last twenty years he has been in the ministry full-time. I rejoice in his growth and honesty with himself and with me.

In my mother's family there are numerous doctors, ministers, leaders and elders in churches. She sought for years to maintain a Christian influence in the home and provide the nurturing she could to the family. I believe the job was too much for her to give what she wanted to give to each of the eight children in our family.

This book is born out of my work with ACAs in my private practice and my own personal recovery. I owe a great deal to the clients I have worked with over the years. They have taught me much. And I'm honored to have been a part of their journey to recovery. Throughout the book I will present statements made by clients. I have changed the names and some of the content to protect their confidentiality.

The book can be divided into five sections: First, chapters one, two and three outline some of the problems ACAs are likely to face and introduce an easy-to-remember recovery format that has proven helpful to many people I work with. Second, chapters four through seven show how the proper use and expression of our feelings are blocked for ACAs, and how we can find healing for our emotions. Third, chapters eight, nine and ten show the damage that is done in the way we think and how we can recover from those unhealthy patterns.

Fourth, chapters eleven, twelve and thirteen focus on behavior, including relationships, and how we can make real changes in the way we act. Chapter fourteen closes the book with a statement of hope and encouragement for the future for all ACAs.

As you move through the book you will see that I start each of the three areas of recovery (feelings, thoughts and behavior) with a chapter or two designed to build awareness. These are then followed by two chapters that offer constructive suggestions for recovery.

For those of you who like shorter books, you will be glad to know that I eliminated a great deal of material from the first manuscript. I was surprised with just how compulsively and perfectionistically I approached the task of writing. Even the act of writing this book has showed me that I am still on my healing journey.

My prayer for you is simply that you can use some of what I've written to add to your recovery process. Take heart, for many ACAs are in recovery and many more will follow.

May God bless your healing journey.

Daryl

1

SURVIVING THE TRAUMA

◆ ◆ ◆

*I*n my family you knew when to ask for things and when not to ask. You had to get what you could immediately. You couldn't believe in any promises for the weekend or a vacation or having friends over next week. Things would always change. Sometimes I wouldn't ask because I knew whatever I wanted just wouldn't work out. Then I began to sneak away and get the things I wanted. I would lie to my parents but then be afraid they would find out what I was doing. I lived by the old saying, "What they don't know won't hurt them." But it seemed I was punished anyway. Even for things that didn't matter. You just never knew when you would get punished or why you were getting punished. It was like living in a constant state of fear watching for a storm to strike. I could even handle the storms better and better as I grew up because at least during those times I knew what to expect. This may sound strange, but I think I can handle a disaster better than I can the little things that happen. *Jean, a forty-year-old ACA*

As he pressed his face against the window, the little six-year-old boy tried to catch a glimpse of his parents as they drove away. His folks thought he was asleep and everything was fine. After all, they would be gone for just a while, they reasoned. The scene was a familiar one for the boy, but the impact remained the same. He was alone and confused. The questions raced in his head: "Would they come back? Why are they leaving? Were they mad at me for not obeying and eating my whole dinner?" The silence was broken only by the noises in the house as the wind blew against the walls. A fear crippled the child but tears were never shown. Time stood still until the lights from the car flashed into his bedroom. He quickly ran and jumped into his bed pretending to be asleep. After the front door opened he could hear fighting, never quite sure what all the noise was about. The fighting produced a relief to abandoned feelings, but brought up other feelings of tension and distrust. As he stated in one session, "I've learned to tolerate relationships based on stress, conflict, distrust and fighting, because at least it meant someone was home. But my panic would slowly build because I knew 'they' would leave again." *Bob, a thirty-five-year-old ACA*

The preceding scene was a familiar one for Bob, a business executive who sought out counseling to deal with his stress and his difficulty in maintaining an intimate relationship. Life seemed to be a constant roller-coaster ride of fear, anger and broken engagements. He would start a relationship with excitement and a new resolve that this one would last. This one would be the person who would make him happy and bring him the love he desired. After a few months, he would be disappointed in his friend, himself and in life. "Where is this thing called love, anyway?" he would ask. His depression and despair for living would signal the end of another relationship.

Bob was unaware that he was recreating his childhood chaos over and over again in adult relationships. The scene he described as a six-year-old boy was one of many that surfaced after several months of therapy. His childhood stresses were the training ground for his style of dealing with intimate relationships. Bob was unaware of what really took place in his family. He had blocked his feelings of fear, panic and insecurity. As a child he had to deny the terror inside him in order to survive. This childhood protection was necessary, but as an adult, the protection would no longer serve him well.

Charlene, a twenty-four-year-old Sunday-school teacher, sought help to cope with her binge-eating. She would make it for a couple of days eating in a "normal" manner, then start to eat as many sweets as she could. Powerless to control herself, she would vomit. Afterward, the feelings of guilt would settle over her like a cloud choking away her life and vitality. She became angry at herself. However, this only led her to repeat her dreaded cycle of binging once again. She began to isolate herself more as each month passed, fearing someone would find out just how she lived. "How could I face my family and friends?" she wondered. "Surely they would be ashamed of me. What if my students found out? I would be a mockery of what I was trying to teach them."

Although raised in a Christian home, Charlene labored under the weight of guilt, never feeling like she was good enough. She was unaware that her eating patterns were a symptom of a diminished self-respect that was taught to her by her parents who themselves were still suffering from the effects of their own childhood traumas.

Adults raised in alcoholic families are often called adult children of alcoholics (ACAs) because they are affected deeply by the trauma. They appear as an adult, but many of the necessary stages of growth were frozen in childhood. And they bear the wounds of childhood into adulthood. For Bob, the parents were both alcoholic and never sought treatment. Today, his parents are dead, victims of the alcohol. Charlene's grandparents were alcoholic. The parents passed on to Charlene the dysfunctional family patterns they learned even though they themselves never drank.

Alcoholism has been coined as the "gift that keeps on giving." For Bob and Charlene and millions of others, it is not a welcome gift, but one that is given nonetheless. The gift is a traumatic childhood that allows ACAs to survive with numerous scars, deep wounds and distortions about the world.

Children raised in an alcoholic or dysfunctional home are children raised with anything from mild to severe overt abuse. Other times the abuse is less obvious such as mental and emotional abuse, neglect, ignoring the child, subtle sexual abuse such as flirting, touching the child inappropriately or stimulating the child sexually.

I remember one adult that recalled his parents teasing him as a boy after he was caught holding his penis. They would say to him things like, "If you like to play with yourself so much, we'll cut it off and hang it around your neck so you can always reach it." The boy was terrified with the possibility of losing this part of his anatomy. He also felt tremendous guilt and shame for touching himself though this was the only part he touched that brought such threats from the parents.

Learning the Rules

Children raised in such homes develop unhealthy thoughts, feelings and behavior. Much of how they live today reflects the way they adapted to the family trauma. Learning the "rules" of the home allowed each person to function within that home.

Some of the common dynamics within dysfunctional families are inconsistency, unpredictability, arbitrariness and chaos (Gravits, Bowden, 1985). Charles L. Whitfield in his book *Healing the Child*

Within presents a classic work on recovery and healing. Some of the following material is adapted from his work.

1. *Inconsistency.* Jean, in the opening vignette of this chapter, commented on how things would always change in her family. A paradox seems to develop in unhealthy families. That which is most consistent is often inconsistency. A person only knows to count on things to change.

While plans and promises can never be certain, some values and ways of relating continue to be consistent. For example, children learn that feelings do not count. They deny what is really happening in the family. What children see in the home is often explained differently than it appeared so that children disown their own view of the family situation. With such messages coming through, it is no wonder that their growth is shut down or hindered. In response to the trauma, children learn to distrust their views of life and build a sense of shame.

2. *Unpredictability.* Children also learn to predict the unpredictable. Since they never know what to expect, they become fearful. Many report that no matter how good things might seem, they were always waiting for something bad to happen. When the home climate was okay, the response was one of anxiety and apprehension wondering, "When will this end?" Another common response is to block feelings because, "One does not want to rock the boat."

3. *Arbitrariness.* The rules for the family become very rigid. But understanding what is really happening is lost. ACAs become perfectionistic which leads to a compulsive style of living. These rules are internalized and provide the structure they need to survive, but not the guidelines for recovery and growth. To grow they would need to be aware of what is happening, but this aware-ness would lead to a violation of the family secrets and be seen as disloyalty which would produce shame.

4. *Chaos.* Whitfield states:

Chaos may be manifested by any of the following: (1)physical or emotional abuse, which teaches the child shame, guilt and "don't feel;" (2) sexual abuse, which teaches the shame, plus distrust and fear of losing control; (3) regular and repeated crises, which teaches a crisis orientation to life; (4) predictable closed communication, which teaches "don't talk," "don't be real," and denial and (5) loss of control, which teaches obsession with being in control, and fusion of loss of boundaries and individuation. (p. 39, 1987)

Like the other common areas, chaos becomes a way of life for the family. Children learn to tolerate very high levels of chaos and stress. And because they have learned to block the feelings this chaos brings, later as an adult it becomes difficult to examine behavior that is inappropriate. What is important to understand is that the adult child seeks out situations that are just as stressful as the home environment, but is not aware that this is the pattern. They seek out the familiar repeatedly.

We're Nebraskan!

Such a reaction is really quite normal. All of us have needs of belonging and acceptance. We want to be part of a group.

I was born and raised in Nebraska. I remember at one parade I wore my Nebraska sweatshirt. All day long people would come up and start a conversation with me. We both wanted to know where in Nebraska we were raised; how long we had been gone from there; did we miss it; have we been back; are there others like us around today? I felt a great urge to run out and buy more sweatshirts and dress in red and white for the rest of my life. I was feeling a sense of bonding and belonging.

The dilemma for adult children is that they tend to wear "clothing" that announces "adult child raised in chaos looking for others with similar roots to recreate our traumatic childhoods." You can bet there won't be much discussion about the heritage each brings, but it will feel "right."

But for adult children "feeling right" probably means a repeat of the chaos and stress. Over and over I've heard people say, "I thought it would be different this time. But he/she was just like the one before." The good news is at least that such people are beginning to develop awareness about the patterns and choices they make. The growth process has begun.

Adult children of alcoholic or dysfunctional families have had to face many difficulties in the home. First, they respond to the "crazy" atmosphere of the family by denying their feelings. Denial is an automatic response to trauma. It protects children from pain and hurt. Denial is one reason ACAs survive. However, distress is still happening within them. Eventually, the symptoms of the distress will manifest themselves in emotional and physical responses such as anxiety, depression, panic attacks, anger, unworthiness, ulcers, headaches, sleep disorders, muscle tension, digestive problems and stress disorders.

Second, ACAs respond to the family atmosphere with changes in the way they think. These thoughts include the rules adopted about themselves, the family, others, the world and God. Some of the common rules adult children believe are:

Feelings are bad.

Do not talk about how you feel.

Do not trust others or yourself.

I'm bad; I'm no good.

I am responsible for Dad's drinking, Mom's pain or the family chaos.

I must be perfect in order to feel good.

If I make a mistake, I'm bad.

Bad people always deserve punishment.

Lastly, ACAs respond with behavior that attempts to control themselves and the world. They develop chemical addictions, compulsive behavior, workaholism, eating disorders, stress disorders, relationship addictions and codependency. Much of the behavior produces short-term relief from the deeper level of unhappiness and bad feelings. However, the long-term effect is more pain and hurt.

Feelings, thoughts and behaviors are the three areas where adult children need recovery and the three areas this book concentrates on in chapters four through twelve. The road to healing intertwines these three. ACAs need emotions healed, thinking patterns clarified and behaviors transformed.

It is simple to tell someone what to do. But to demonstrate how to produce healing and wholeness within is quite another matter. The thrust of this book is to provide foundational tools that will assist an ACA's recovery. These tools can be used in connection with other recovery choices such as therapy, group work, support groups, church activities and family contacts.

Imperfect Saints

Some churches deny that the problems in ACAs exist. This inhibits growth, so a final note is appropriate here. No one would challenge the idea that churches are made up of imperfect people in need of spiritual wholeness and healing. Yet often the thrust of many ministries changes over time from acceptance to perfectionism. The message that people need to appear as saints in all parts of their lives begins to characterize some teaching and preaching. At first, the admission to being a sinner in need of a savior is welcomed and acceptance begins to permeate the new believer. But lifestyle changes are slow in coming for most ACAs. And as they look around, they struggle to find believers that have any "real" sins. It looks like the other members of the group are so much more "spiritual" and "sin-free."

Since such new believers want to be included in the group, they act as if "it is all okay" with them. Yet, deep inside there is a pain, hurt and an uncomfortableness. Over time, a gap begins to develop between what is seen outside and what is happening inside. As this gap begins to widen, ACAs once again experience an inner tension. To provide relief from this stress, the deepest-held coping skills are utilized: denial, blocking of feelings and compulsive behaviors.

These coping skills are used to adapt to a new belief system and new rules for living. However, the rules have a special meaning to the adult child. They are messages that mirror past confusion, chaos and lack of safety in the family. Adult children are traumatized again, this time within the church family. There, they may find standards of perfectionism, double messages about personal acceptance and self-denial, and confusion about God's will and their personal will. They may misunderstand an attack by a leader against sinful behavior as a personal attack. Some messages given in the church may sound familiar to an adult child—feelings do not count, do not trust in yourself and never question those in authority.

The adult child will suffer spiritually simply because the growth cycle is once again stuck, just like it was in the home. Wholeness remains just beyond reach. ACAs act more religious, appear more together and seem to be maturing, but they are still children within.

Like a family, the church has the potential to meet the inner needs of safety, acceptance, love, belonging, forgiveness and growth each person possesses.

Let each of us strive to "know the truth" and break through our denial. May we be "set free" to be drawn to a healing lifestyle rather than stuck in a punishing lifestyle that leaves us looking good and feeling terrible. It is my earnest prayer as you go through the following chapters that God's comforting power will help soothe the pain. I pray that he will reveal his truth to you and enable you to have courage to grow and heal.

2
ROADBLOCKS ON THE HEALING JOURNEY
♦ ♦ ♦

*I*just begin to shake inside. It's like something awful is going to happen and I have to be on guard every minute. It feels like I could go out-of-control and totally be embarrassed. If they knew how I felt or even saw me "lose-it," I would be devastated. I could never attend church there again. My husband's ministry would be ruined, and we would never get another placement in the church. Who wants to hire someone with a "crazy" wife. I keep up a front most of the time but feel I'm one breath away from a breakdown. The pressure builds inside me. I need a rest but just can't say no to the requests made upon me. I feel guilty if I say no, but I feel pressure inside when I say yes. There just isn't enough time to get all of the things done I've agreed to do. I vow I'll cut back my activities but I just can't. And now I feel so tired and exhausted. I don't have the energy to keep up much longer. I feel guilty even talking to you because I know I shouldn't feel this way, and there are so many people that really need help. I know I should just trust more in the Lord and all this would go away. Why can't I just live like I know I should? Like any Christian should? *Cindy, forty-year-old ACA*

Being raised in a dysfunctional home seems to encourage thinking, feeling and behaving in extremes. One extreme many ACAs believe is that change must be immediate. This leads to frustration when we fail in large or small ways. Recovery, however, is a journey. This chapter focuses on some roadblocks ACAs will face as they travel their recovery path. The journey of recovery is usually started because we are tired of our current lifestyle and its pain. We finally get "sick and tired" of being "sick and tired."

Herein lies a dilemma. I want to change and I believe that I should change, but I am locked into patterns. I only know what I know to this point in my life. And if what I know what has brought me pain and dysfunction, how do I get beyond myself?

Change Is Possible

Furthermore, I've already established a comfort zone that gives me safety. It is what I depend on and count on to provide structure to my life. Even if this comfort zone produces heartache and misery, it is all I know. To move beyond it increases my anxiety. As the fears grow I retreat back to my comfort zone. The momentary safety of the familiar gives way to frustrations and pain. I become defeated and discouraged and conclude that I'll never be different. I'll never be what I can be. And it does not matter, anyway, because change is something others can do but I'll never accomplish.

So the cycle repeats itself over and over. But deep within each of us lies the sense that re-emerges time and time again that we want something different. The need for recovery is characterized by the sense "it could be better" and "something is missing."

Because of the tendency to think, feel and act in extremes, adult children often approach recovery with an all-or-nothing perfectionism. The goals established are quite high and the deadline for reaching those goals is usually immediate. They become disillusioned quickly when attempts to change are not successful. The inner conflict that becomes a way of life is reminiscent of the apostle Paul's struggle. He said, "I do not understand what I do. For what I want to do I do not do, but what I hate I do" (Romans 7:15).

He also wrote in 2 Corinthians 3:17-18, "Where the Spirit of the Lord is, there is freedom. And we, who with unveiled faces all reflect the Lord's glory, are being transformed into his likeness with ever-increasing glory, which comes from the Lord, who is the Spirit." These verses have helped me to change my ideas about the growth process.

First, where the Spirit is, is freedom. The idea that God releases me rather than puts me in bondage was new to me.

Second, each of us as believers reflects the glory of God. This seemed to go against my perfectionism. I thought I had to become perfect and be sin-free in order to be loved by God and reflect God.

Third, we are being transformed into a greater likeness of the image of Christ. God gives us a transforming experience. I struggled with the idea of performing, but God is wanting me to be patient with the process of inner healing that he has started. I did not believe all of this at first. However, over time the truth slowly became a part of me.

Recovering in order to gain acceptance from others merely repeats our childhood of perfectionism and approval-seeking from our parents. The process of recovery is possible because we are accepted by God. It is to be experienced in a daily living that is full of victories and failures. As Rainier Maria Rilke wrote,

Be patient toward all that is unsolved
   in your heart . . .

Try to love the questions themselves . . .

Do not now seek the answers,
  which cannot be given
  because you would not be able
to live them.

And the point is,
  to live everything.
Live the questions now.
Perhaps you will then
  gradually,
  without noticing it,
Live along some distant day
into the answers.

Myths about the Journey

During the process of healing, ACAs are certain to encounter frustrations which are like the roadblocks which often slow down any journey. However, on the journey to healing, these roadblocks take the form of myths in our thinking. So there is no need for a lengthy detour if the myths can be identified. The following is a list of eleven such myths and the explanations which remove them as roadblocks.

Myth 1. One should forget the past and only focus upon what's happening today. Adult children have learned to survive extremely difficult situations. One of the survival tools used most frequently is denial. Subconsciously, adult children coped with the childhood trauma by blocking the feelings they had. At the time the use of denial was very appropriate. But now adult children need to honestly examine the past to gain insight into the present. Someone once said, "The truth will set you free, but first it will make you miserable." It is difficult but necessary to acknowledge the past to develop an awareness of who you are today. It's also been said, "That of which we are unaware, we rarely change." Recovery involves looking at today and yesterday.

——Myth 2. Change is something that must be immediate. I have known people who had a conversion experience that totally turned their lives around. I have seen people in a moment of insight change the course of their lives from destructive choices to healthy choices. But these individuals are rare. Most of us will progress slowly in the healing journey.

Believing that change must be immediate is born out of our perfectionistic childhood thinking. Adult children tend to think in a mythical all-or-nothing format. This sets us up for defeat. Since most change is not immediate, we fail. After the failure we conclude we will never change. And then it is back to the comfort zone. We need to adopt the idea that healing takes time and commit ourselves to the personal responsibility of participating in our healing process. Learning to celebrate small steps becomes a gift that we give to ourselves in the recovery process.

Myth 3. Only the past determines the future. Many adult children were taught that "you can't teach an old dog new tricks." We have been taught to believe the myth that what we are and who we are will never change. It is true that the early teaching and experiences we encountered have a profound effect upon us. But within each of us lies the capacity to grow and alter the way we act and feel.

The message of the New Testament is that change is possible. Paul said we can "be transformed by the renewing of your mind" (Romans 12:2) and "live up to what we have already attained" (Philippians 3:16). Peter said, "Add to your faith goodness; and to goodness, knowledge; and to knowledge, self-control; and to self-control, perseverance; and to perseverance, godliness; and to godliness, brotherly kindness; and to brotherly kindness, love" (2 Peter 1:5-7). If only the past determines what I will always be, then the encouragement to change found in Scripture is meaningless.

As an exercise, write an extremely practical note to yourself listing the things you are doing differently today than last year. Perhaps you are wearing a different hairstyle, learning to play chess, shopping at a new store, living someplace new, working at a different job, adjusting to the addition of a new family member or driving a car that has a 5-speed transmission instead of an automatic. Changes may be both uncomfortable and encouraging. Often we are changing a great deal more than we give ourselves any credit for.

Myth 4. If something is worth doing, it's worth doing well. Explode this myth by saying, "If something is worth doing, it's worth doing in small steps." Let me illustrate. We all believe learning to walk is worthwhile, so let's visit a family scene where a child is taking the first steps in a long life of walking. The parent holds the child up with the child's arms stretched out and tiny feet barely touching the floor. Other family members are sitting around as cheerleaders. The child leans forward. The parent lets go. The child steps forward and falls. A celebration occurs. Cheering and loud noise fill the house.

"He's walking."

"Good boy!"

"Somebody call the grandparents, the neighbors, the . . . the . . . the president."

Now by our standards of walking, the child failed. One step, what's all the fuss about?

Change and growth rely on the celebration of any movement toward the desired goal. Walking is worth doing, and it's done poorly at first. But celebrating the child's step assures other steps to follow. Recovery is celebrating the steps of growth, even those done poorly because the goals of recovery and feeling better and making wiser choices are worth doing.

Myth 5. God's forgiveness is fine for everyone but me. A key roadblock for most ACAs is the sense of being unforgiven. While growing up, forgiveness was rarely modeled. Conflicts were not resolved and each member was left with a sense of blame and the feelings of shame. ACAs had to be perfect. Children have flaws, yet mistakes were not acceptable. So the children learn to perform in order to be approved. As an adult the performance continues. ACAs approach God under the influence of this myth. "I must do all that he asks of me or I'm no good. If I make a mistake, there exists no forgiveness, just punishment."

ACA spend a great amount of energy criticizing and rebuking every imperfection. Although intellectually they can read about God's forgiveness, emotionally it just does not feel "right." Many are left with years of bitterness and resentment that blocks the healing process. ACAs need to fellowship with believers who daily practice love, acceptance and forgiveness. In this way they will begin to experience what forgiveness really means.

Many ACAs take one of two approaches when forgiving others. First, they may stuff the feelings and appear to be forgiving while in fact they are denying the situation and enabling the other person to continue to act inappropriately.

A second approach is holding on to bitterness. ACAs tend to get upset about everything that happens. It does not matter whether the event or situation is big or small. They fight because the leftover hurts from the past have not been touched with forgiveness. The silent cry of ACAs is for the soothing grace forgiveness can bring.

Myth 6. If I turned everything over to God, I would not have the problems I have now. All of us have tried to let God take over everything and still found ourselves hurting, confused and making destructive choices. God is not a magician who removes all of our pain, sorrow and difficulties. Sometimes answers to life's problems are confusing. Sometimes there is no ultimate answer. We need to learn to embrace all of life, including the ambiguity, the confusion and the pain.

God supplies us with power, comfort in pain, a guiding vision, a structure for living and healing for the soul. But he never promised us a life that would be free of pain. An older man once said to me, "God doesn't promise peace from the storms of life, but rather that we can have peace amidst the storms." The apostle Paul said, "I have learned to be content whatever the circumstances. I know what it is to be in need, and I know what it is to have plenty. I have learned the secret of being content in any and every situation" (Philippians 4:11-12).

Learning to turn ourselves over to God is a reflection of our needs, our imperfections and the flawed world we live in. Fellowship with God will allow us to develop a broader vision about our life. But to believe the myth that he will remove everything painful makes God a drug. The modern-day preachers of pain-free living ignore the reality of everyday life.

Myth 7. I must be able to do what I should do to be healed. If I cannot, there is something wrong with me. Over and over while growing up adult children were made to feel stupid, inadequate, bad and guilty for their actions and feelings. In this way the parents passed on to them the messages they received from their parents.

One of the legacies of the dysfunctional home is negative self-worth or shame. This myth creates a double burden. One is that I must know how to grow and change. The second is that I'm bad if I do not know how to do this. Instead of learning the skills needed to be free from the past and heal, ACAs are thrust into the past by feelings of badness and shame. The difference is that now the devaluing is being done by ACAs and not by the parent. This is the self-view that I internalized from my family. In recovery, we must suspend our constant self-criticism and invalidation and learn the new skills that we need to heal and make positive choices.

Myth 8. External events and other people must change or I'll never be able to be healed. Children normally look to the significant people in their lives, such as parents, for a sense of value, acceptance, love and belonging. Children learn about themselves from the messages sent by their parents. Eventually they grow and seek independence. Later a personal identity is developed. This identity is partially the internalizing of the parent's messages. It is also the conclusions they have drawn through self-evaluation and life experience.

In a family where the messages are invalidating and confusing, this process hits a roadblock. The children do not fully learn to trust themselves, take appropriate risks, establish independence and autonomy, and later form an inner-directed identity. As adults, ACAs believe the myth that the change must take place in others. They want other people to confirm things in them that should have beem validated by their parents. Since adult children are drawn to people raised in similar homes, they are trying to get validation from people who are looking to them for the same thing. It is no wonder that neither party is satisfied.

In recovery our inner-focus is reclaimed. This is especially necessary because the others around us may never change. Christian ACAs are bothered a great deal by the concept of being inner-directed. Yet, if we are to respond to the healing work of God within us, we need to be responsive to our inner self. The old adage is still true today, "A better world begins with me."

Myth 9. God will be just like my human father. While there will be exceptions, children develop a view of God based on the relationship they have with their parents. In particular, fathers have a tremendous impact on the experience ACAs expect when approaching God.

On a recent drive home from work I was listening to a religious radio talk show covering the topic of abuse and runaways. A caller told a story of multiple assaults and sexual abuse by her father and some of his male friends. Then the moderator of the show asked the caller to pray, turn her life over to God and begin a personal relationship with God. The caller, a young girl around twelve to fourteen years old, blurted out, "I can't do that." Then in a voice broken by her sobbing she said, "I . . . can't . . . do that because Jesus was . . . a man . . . and

God will . . . be like my father." I was moved by the hurt she faced and her fear of turning her life over to "another man." I believe she captures the point of this roadblock.

There are several ways alcoholic parents affect the image ACAs have about God. ACAs faced physical and emotional abandonment in the home. So they may view God as being absent. They also usually could not approach their parents with problems. So they may view God as coldly indifferent, distant and unloving. ACAs may view God as punishing because, as a child, they learned to fear an inconsistent and punitive father. Oftentimes, they were judged by unrealistic and inappropriate standards. They learned to anticipate being criticized and judged. This can lead to believing that God is always angry at them.

ACAs may think God demands perfection. As children they were expected to make no mistakes. Thus, being loved by God becomes a conditional agreement. They think, "If I measure up, God will love me; if I don't, I deserve punishment." ACAs may view God as if he was not to be trusted. This is because they learned to mistrust their fathers who were impulsive, chaotic and unpredictable. ACAs develop a strong desire to be self-reliant and overcontrolling. After all, surviving the home depends on the child's ability to live without close relationships. So trust, a fundamental ingredient to establishing healthy relationships, whether with God or other people, is damaged.

ACAs have difficulty expressing feelings of joy since they grew up repressing playfulness and spontaneity. A relationship with God tends to mirror this experience. Life is serious, so the ACA develops the same attitude in the spiritual life.

ACAs have difficulty believing God wants to comfort, nurture, heal and support them. Yet many of the promises in the Bible reflect a supportive, caring and present God. As ACAs heal they usually begin to modify their distortions about God and his promises.

Myth 10. Others must approve of my actions or I'm no good. I once read "needing approval is a basic childhood need, that one never out-grows." I think we all like to be accepted and appreciated for who we are and what we do. The problem comes when we do not get approval from others and draw the conclusion that we must be bad. This is a result of being raised in a family that promoted shame.

When we are attempting to change and choose a healthier path, we need all the encouragement we can get. But what often happens? People around us make fun of our changes, laugh at our attempts to improve, put down our insights, ridicule the goals we have and get angry that we want something better. This feels like home again. So we put ourselves down and feel bad, just as we did as a child. Then we either get very fearful or very angry. But we tend to stop our attempts to change.

Once again, we make peace by retreating to the style that we know best. If I was trying to quit using alcohol, I use it instead. If I was trying to get close to people, I distance myself. If I was trying to be more communicative, I clam up. If I tried to develop more spirituality, I abandon God. I retreat from whatever I was risking. But I still feel bad.

Recovery is learning that I am the greatest critic of myself. What others did in disapproving of me only triggered the personal disapproval I already had. Learning to let go of this constant self-devaluation is part of recovery.

Myth 11. It is selfish and bad to focus on myself. Others count more than I do. A book could be written on this topic alone. Parents that teach this concept restrict their children to a life that is confused and solely other-directed. Recovery, however, does not mean we replace other-centered living with only self-centered living. Recovery means seeking a balance between what I want, feel and need and what others want, feel and need. This balance allows for flexibility in making decisions in interpersonal relationships. There are times when what I want takes precedence over others' needs. And there are times when what others want takes precedence over my needs.

Our difficulty lies in an either-or mentality. This leads to a rigid style that limits how I will act no matter what the circumstances are. Recovery of balance brings value to me and to others. They count and so do I. Others are responsible, but so am I. Others have needs and so do I. One is not more important than the other because both have value and worth before the Creator. There are three primary relationships in life: with God, with others and with myself. Learning to balance these relationships is an essential component of recovery.

Many churches teach that self-denial and self-assertion are opposites that cannot exist together. The truth is that they represent two sides of a coin. We need both in our life. There are times we must be courageous and bold, take action about harmful situations, speak up and voice our opinion, take a stand for health, goodness and holiness. But we have been taught that anything relating to ourselves is selfish. This is not balanced. Not only should I care for others, it is also my job to take care of myself and the responsibility for my feelings, thoughts and behaviors.

Most ACAs survive great trauma from their homelife. They begin the journey of healing because the leftover pain can no longer be contained by denial. But there are roadblocks that interrupt this healing journey. These roadblocks lie on the pathways of self, others and God. Exposing them as myths encourages adult children of alcoholics to persevere and stay on the recovery path they have chosen.

3
THE AAA RECOVERY FORMAT

◆ ◆ ◆

I can't understand why Dad treated me like he did. All I ever wanted was for him to be proud of me and tell me he loved me. It just doesn't make sense. Now I want to stop the crazy stuff in my own life. But I don't know how. I'm tired of feeling depressed and scared. I feel empty inside like I don't know who I am. It's like "there's nobody home." I don't know how to act.

When something happens to me at work I don't know if I'm supposed to get angry or just shut up. Afterward, I feel tension in my shoulders and I get a stomachache. Pretty silly isn't it. I know I'm a good worker, but nobody seems to care. It's like I can never do enough. I stay late. I take work home. But, I get passed over for promotions, and then I just get a bad feeling all over me. I spend my time off figuring out what's wrong so I can fix it. But nothing seems to work out.

I attended a stress-management workshop that the company provided for us. The instructor told us to "relax." The only thing I felt was anger at the instructor and then I felt bad because I should relax more.

On top of work my church activities really keep me going too. There's not enough time to fulfill my obligations. When I show up late for a function, I really feel guilty. Sometimes people make fun of me for being late. Or if I couldn't be there, I would hear things like, "What was so important that you couldn't attend last night?" I know they mean well but when I hear them say I have my priorities all messed up, I just feel terrible. I vow I'll do better and work harder. But sometimes I don't know what's most important. I guess they are right. I don't have good priorities for my life. So I make a list, but the list is so full I never get enough time to do it all. My vacations are spent just trying to get things caught up that I know I need to do.   *Anna, a thirty-five-year-old adult child*

Adults raised in dysfunctional homes use denial to survive their childhood. However, Anna's experience shows that these survival skills break down leaving a life characterized by a host of painful symptoms. Recovery begins when the pain breaks through the denial and demands to be resolved.

The Leakage Theory

Surviving childhood can be like stuffing garbage into bags and hiding them in the garage every day. After years of filling bags and stacking them, the garage gets full. We have to compress them to allow for more bags. Some of them break, become untied or wear out. But we still fill the garage with garbage. We notice a smell coming from the garage. Something needs to be done, but we do not know what to do. Still, we squeeze in more garbage. The smell increases. We continue to compress the bags and fill the garage.

Eventually a black, slimy fluid oozes out of the stack and flows under the door. It travels outside, down the driveway. We clean up the mess. We spray the garage with scents to destroy the smell. It still stinks. We clean again. We stuff more bags. We spray, clean, stuff and become more angry, frustrated and discouraged. "Where will this end?" we ask. We clean up again, filling more bags with garbage. These bags leak more of the dark substance. Our lives become organized around keeping the stuff in the garage from affecting the beauty and odor of our house. But we cannot keep the bags from leaking.

Finally, we start our recovery process because the pain and hurts can no longer be contained and "cleaned up."

It is never too late to begin the healing of our pain and trauma. We spent most of our lives running from our pain, hiding from our pain, avoiding our pain and replacing it with other things. This can only relieve the pain for a short time. Healing will not begin until we look into our childhood family, become aware of the pain it created in us and understand the strategies we use to protect against that pain. That is the first step in a simple, three-part recovery concept that I will refer to throughout this book. It is what I call the AAA recovery format.

Triple-A

The bumpers of many cars display the American Automobile Association sticker. It is an oval surrounding three A's. This advertises an automobile club, but you can use it as a reminder of three key recovery principles:

A—Awareness

A—Acceptance

A—Action

Awareness. Just as in the story of the leaking garbage, recovery starts when we become aware of our problems, feelings, confusion and helplessness. The less we deny, the more we become aware. But without our defense mechanism of denial, we begin to feel the pain from our childhood. One of my clients broke through her guard of denial only to discover that she was a victim of sexual abuse as a child. The feelings she experienced were as real as if the abuse had happened last week. But having identified her problem, she was then able to develop appropriate strategies to heal the wounds within her and make constructive choices for herself.

Most recovery support groups use the 12-step program conceived by Alcoholics Anonymous. The first step is to admit we have no power over our own lives. The next step is to admit our need for God. We must be honest about our feelings and our weakness. Then, like the psalmist of old, we need to "cry aloud to the LORD . . . lift up our voice . . . pour out our complaints and tell him our trouble" (Psalm 142:1-2).

Awareness is an ongoing process that exposes our true hurts, pains and needs. We need to understand our families and the repeating chaotic patterns in our lives. Chapters four, five, eight and eleven will be especially helpful as you seek to build awareness of your feelings, thoughts and behaviors.

Acceptance. As children, we learned to deny our feelings and the problems we faced. We learned to reject ourselves and criticize ourselves constantly. The family conveyed messages to us that we were not important and should not be ourselves. We did not trust others and we did not trust ourselves. In the AAA recovery model, acceptance has two meanings. First, it is believing in reality. It is essential to break through our denial and honestly look at how we escape the problems we actually face.

Jacqui Lee Schiff (1975) identified four levels of emotional discounting that protect us from confronting potentially damaging emotional situations:

1. We discount the existence of a problem. We act as if there is no problem.

☐ The adult child that was physically abused says, "I had a normal childhood."

☐ The family returns from church only to find daddy passed out in the bathroom and nobody says anything.

2. We discount the significance of a problem, and play down its importance or intensity. While at best recognizing a problem exists, the impact of it is minimized.

☐ The anorexic mother comments to her children, "I've gained a pound and things are better." All the while she and her family deny the terror they feel about her life-threatening condition.

☐ "Everyone in our family was edgy: that's just the way we are."

3. We discount the possibility of solving a problem. Because we believe nothing can be done about it, we do not expect to do anything about it.

☐ "I just could not live without him," said a woman whose husband was a violent alcoholic.

☐ "If I have to tell you what I need, that means you do not care about me."

4. We discount our own abilities and blame ourselves. Someone else may be able to handle the problem, but "I can't." This is self-shaming, not self-changing. You feel bad, but the problem still exists.

☐ "I'm bad."

☐ "I'm too nervous, too old, too busy, etc."

☐ "I'll never learn."

This first meaning of acceptance is to battle against the discounting messages ACAs use to survive. It is learning to say, "There is a problem," "My behaviors aren't helping the situation," "I do have feelings," "Hiding hasn't solved the problems," "It is my responsibility to heal, or change my feelings, thoughts and behaviors in order to recover."

The second meaning of acceptance is to provide comfort. As we feel comfort, we can become secure enough to confront the critical messages we've heard our whole life. We can start sending ourselves messages that we count, that we are important, that we do have value and worth.

In a dysfunctional family, everyone learns to blame and feel shame. Alcoholic families are often labeled "shame-based" families. If we felt confused, we felt bad. If we felt angry, we felt bad. If we felt afraid, we felt bad. If we made a mistake or were blamed for the way we acted, we felt bad. The feeling of badness is the same as shame. (Shame is an important issue that we will look at in more depth in chapter six.)

Shame-based individuals are very critical of themselves. Because the shame is developed so early in childhood and becomes so familiar, it feels like the "real me." The sense of shame becomes toxic because it devalues us for the rest of our lives. Our toxic sense of self is then bonded to every feeling we have and everything we do. We simply cannot escape the constant sense of badness and the repetitive devaluing statements we make.

Shame impairs all my attempts to heal my wounded heart, grieve my losses, and change my behavior patterns. Shame interferes with our attempts to fellowship with God and impairs all our relationships. Like the psalmist, we look for sympathy and comforters (Psalm 69:20).

In recovery our sense of trust grows and our healthy shame returns, a sense of our human limitation emerges. It is the feeling we have when vulnerability is exposed. We really are not perfect. And there will always be situations that happen that catch us unprepared.

As the trust builds and the feeling of health returns within us, we can dismantle the unrealistically high expectations that we had of ourselves from childhood. The moral standard we have can be balanced with realism and used as the guide it was intended to be.

Without healing our shame, any time we break even the smallest part of our own moral code we condemn ourselves and retreat to feeling bad. This is inappropriate guilt. Healthy guilt is the feeling that alerts us that we are truly doing something morally wrong rather than missing our own arbitrary standards.

Let us not confuse acceptance with an attitude that we will necessarily like or approve of what we discover about ourselves. It doesn't mean we want to stay stuck where we find ourselves. As awareness builds, a natural response is sadness, grieving and anger at what we find. But the paradox of recovery is simply stated—until we can accept (face whatever is reality) and comfort (remove the issue of toxic shame, my badness) we will never be free to move into consistent, productive behavior patterns.

Action. It is human nature to want to fix our problems, ourselves and the pain we feel. But most ACAs try repeatedly to change situations by taking steps that do not promote healing. We act in the same manner we always have and are continually defeated. It has been said, "Insanity is doing the same thing and expecting different results."

Early actions attempt to break the rules of "Don't feel," "Don't trust," and "Don't talk." We may take the action of talking about what happened and how we feel to a supportive group. The love and acceptance mirrored back to us helps in our healing and encourages us to reach out more.

Early recovery steps are primarily discovering ourselves and reconstructing a network around us that enhances our recovery work. The steps may be to contact a support group, a therapist, a meeting of Adult Children of Alcoholics, a church family, or attending meetings and workshops which build strategies for healing work. It may be a time of looking within to discover more about ourselves, or looking at our family more closely to understand family patterns. Or it may be considering the ways we continue to produce self-defeating behavior. Whatever route it takes, the early action steps are intended to build awareness, produce understanding, build comfort strategies, live honestly, take responsibility for one's own recovery path, stop escape behaviors, free oneself from the bondage of the past and build a daily recovery program.

The old adage "Nothing changes, if nothing changes" is true for all of us. For ACAs risking new behaviors requires a great deal of risk. However, if we do not risk changing our actions, we will recreate the same strategies we've always used.

This AAA format gives simple, daily direction to recovery work. It can be used in the early recovery process as well as when one has pursued recovery work for months or years. We will always need to build honest awareness, accept ourselves without shame and take constructive action.

A Family Awareness Exercise

Recovery for adult children of alcoholics starts with the awareness of the family of origin. In this section, I would like you to begin this process by answering a few questions about your childhood. There are no "right" answers to these questions. They are simply intended to stimulate awareness about your family. If you have done intensive family-of-origin work, this exercise may seem too elementary. Others may feel uncomfortable as you look at your family for the first time. Take heart, remember you are not alone. We all need to look honestly at our roots. I am not asking you to assign blame for your problems. Instead, use these questions to take a good look at your experiences of family life as a child. Feel free to get a piece of paper or a notebook and take time right now to write down a sentence or paragraph answer to the following questions.

☐ What was it like to live in my family?
☐ How would I describe my father?
☐ How would I describe my mother?
☐ How would I describe my grandparents?
☐ How would I describe my siblings?
☐ Who was the safest for me?
☐ Who was the most difficult for me?
☐ What role did alcohol play in my family?
☐ What secrets could I not share with anyone else? *(I did not*

answer this for a long time. When I finally did I used a code so no one would know my answer.)

☐ What were some messages or rules I remember, rules such as, "Don't talk" or "Don't feel"?

☐ What do I remember feeling as a child in my family?

☐ What did I do to cope in my family, such as keeping quiet or taking care of Mom?

☐ In what way is my adult life similar to my childhood family?

☐ In what way is my adult life different from my childhood family?

☐ As a child, what were the things I said I would never do as an adult?

☐ What were some losses I experienced as a child, such as a pet?

After you have answered these questions, pause. Sit back. Take a few deep breaths. Take a break. Feelings may have been stirred up within which show a part of you needs attention. Recovery is a process and on each step of the journey we need comfort and safety. Decide what you need right now and give yourself permission to do it. Find a comforting friend. Talk with a pastor. Confide in your partner. Listen to some music. Remember the AAA format.

A God of Comfort

Once, as I was working on my recovery I read 2 Corinthians 1. In that chapter I learned three important lessons about comfort. Paul says, "Praise be to the God and Father of our Lord Jesus Christ, the Father of compassion and the God of all comfort, who comforts us in all our troubles, so that we can comfort those in any trouble with the comfort we ourselves have received from God" (2 Corinthians 1:3-4). These verses were life-giving to me.

First, I learned that God is a God of compassion and comfort. I used to view God as an angry, upset God who was not interested in my troubles. I thought he wanted me to shape up. Instead, the Bible showed me that he is a God of comfort for each of us. He brings us people who, if we suffer, they suffer with us. If we are honored, they rejoice with us (1 Corinthians 14:26). My view of God slowly changed over the years to see him as caring for my healing and my sense of wholeness.

Second, he "comforts us in all our troubles." He wants us to develop safety, peace and gentleness with ourselves. People will always have troubles. We live in a fallen world, we have imperfect parents and have an adversary that seeks to destroy us. God does not want us to be left with condemnation but with comfort. In 2 Corinthians 2:7-8, Paul is discussing a member of the church in Corinth who was involved in serious sin. "You ought to forgive and comfort him," he tells the Corinthians, "so that he will not be overwhelmed by excessive sorrow. I urge you, therefore, to reaffirm your love for him." We too need to reaffirm our love for ourselves and find supportive people that will reaffirm love for us. We are comforted by God, ourselves and others.

Third, we are able to comfort others with the comfort we have received. This shows that we have passed through a healing process. It demonstrates real recovery because we are used by God to help in the healing process of others. The comfort we give to others is we received from God when we were troubled. We forgive because we have been forgiven. We love because we have been loved. We are gentle with others because we have felt the gentleness given to us. We are compassionate because we have experienced compassion.

It was once said, "If each of us knew the real history of everyone we met, we would feel compassion and understanding for every person." If we really knew the pain, hurt, trauma, chaos, confusion, fear and path the other person walked, we would begin to understand them better.

I believe the same applies to ourselves. We need to become aware of our pain, trauma, chaos and confusion to gain understanding and compassion for ourselves. There is no real lasting change in ourselves without awareness. But gaining the awareness is painful. This is why comfort and compassion are so important. I will only repeat my past and recreate my family-of-origin lifestyle unless I break free. Breaking free is painful and God stands ready to help us by acceptance, compassion and comfort. We will address comfort and acceptance again later, but let me restate this concept. We need to forgive and comfort ourselves so we will not be overwhelmed by excessive sorrow. We need to reaffirm our love for ourselves.

4
DISCOVERING
OUR EMOTIONS

♦ ♦ ♦

I don't know what's wrong with me. My wife says I should feel more but I just don't understand what she is talking about. It just feels like a pressure builds up inside of me and then I get real angry. But most of the time I feel numb, sort of closed off on the inside. I want to tell her more about myself but when I think about talking with her I just get a weird feeling inside. Then I avoid the whole issue entirely. **Ken**

Feelings are greatly misunderstood. Most of us minimize the importance of how feelings affect us. Very early in my spiritual training I heard the concept that life is like a train. The engine was the facts, the coal car was my faith and the caboose was my feelings. The analogy went something like this: "If faith follows facts, then feelings will come along as well. But if you put your feelings first, then the train won't go right."

Many times I've heard pastors and ministers say with great anger that if we ever felt bad after believing in Christ's saving work, we did not have enough faith or a sincere desire to serve God. Adult children who hear these messages can become stuck in their spiritual development.

What adult children really hear from these messages is that it is important to cut themselves off from feelings and not trust their own reactions. They believe that their lack of warm feelings for God makes them deficient. They should try harder to get it "right." What they hear is similar to what they heard in their family of trauma. These messages foster more denial, and do not provide the acceptance and love the ACAs so desperately need to develop.

This chapter explores some of the prominent feelings ACAs carry with them from their childhood. The goal of this chapter is to build awareness about our emotional side.

Feelings Are Biblical

I believe many Christians do not understand that a sound mind and healthy emotions are both important. There are numerous examples from the Bible where feelings played an important role in the growth process and reflected spiritual experience.

My guilt has overwhelmed me
    like a burden too heavy to bear.
My wounds fester and are loathsome
    because of my sinful folly.
I am bowed down and brought very
    low; all day long I go about mourning.
My back is filled with searing pain;
    there is no health in my body.
I am feeble and utterly crushed; I groan
    in anguish of heart. (Psalm 38:4-8)

This psalm is rich in emotion. And what did the psalmist do with these innermost feelings? "All my longings lie open before you, O Lord; my sighing is not hidden from you" (Psalm 38:9). He felt the feelings and expressed them to God. This is exactly the point of early recovery. The pain we feel presses us to take notice. We have to be honest with it and take appropriate action.

Adam and Eve experienced fear and did what most of us do today—they hid. "But the LORD God called to the man, 'Where are you?' He answered, 'I heard you in the garden, and I was afraid because I was naked; so I hid' " (Genesis 3:9-10). The feeling of fear was normal and appropriate given the circumstances. What I find refreshing is the open dialog. Adam expressed clearly what he did and what he felt. Later, he tried to shift the responsibility, but here he described accurately to God what he felt and did.

When Jesus' dear friend Lazarus died, Jesus was glad, troubled and deeply moved, which he expressed by weeping (John 11:14, 33, 35, 38). In the Garden of Gethsemane just before his arrest and crucifixion, Jesus felt sorrow (Matthew 26:38). The letter to the Hebrews records that Jesus was tempted just like us. It says, "For we do not have a high priest who is unable to sympathize with our weaknesses, but we have one who has been tempted in every way, just as we are—yet was without sin" (Hebrews 4:15). How does this verse cause us to respond? The writer continues in the next verse, "Let us then approach the throne of grace with confidence."

Feelings Are Human

Is it wrong to feel angry? Is it bad to feel sad? Should I ever feel depressed? Am I never supposed to feel anxiety? Am I stupid to feel hurt?

Now ask yourself some more questions. Is it right to feel joy? Excitement? Happiness? Peace? Security? The list could go on, but how did you do? Did you find yourself labeling some emotions as bad and some as good?

If you did, you're pretty normal. That is what most of us learned. In the mind of the child the world is polarized as good and bad. And feelings are just like that. Some are experienced as bad and some are good. What we attempt to do with our feelings is get rid of the "bad ones" and only leave the "good ones." But in the process of trying to keep feelings away from us we exhaust ourselves of the energy we need to live day-by-day. This is like trying to hold several inflated balloons under water. The moment we let go, they surface and we have to struggle to submerge them again.

Feelings are part of being human. They exist to give flavor to life. Some are painful and some are pleasurable. But they do exist. The more feelings are preached against, the more we will tend to deny and suppress our feelings. In the process, we become less than whole. We are created as whole creatures that have a unifying, integrating person made up of body, mind, soul, emotions, will and more. Feelings are not right or wrong. Certainly they can lead to destructive acts and create unhealthy stress to the body. But the notion that feelings are bad misses the point. Feelings actually help us in many ways.

Feelings Are Signals

When we drive a car, we rely on our gauges to give us information. We have an oil pressure gauge, a fuel indicator and a temperature gauge. When the oil light goes on, it could mean that the pressure is low, there is a small oil leak, there is a short in the electrical system, the oil level is low or the oil pan fell off 100 yards back down the road. One thing for sure, something's going on and I need to check it out.

The one wrong response would be to say the light is not on. For example, after noticing the light is on I may try to not look at the dashboard, reasoning to myself that there is not a problem. After all, I serviced the car just last week. I might cover the annoying little light with a piece of tape. Or, worse, I could grasp my shoe and hit the dash until the light goes out. There, that's better. No light, so everything must be OK. That is, everything is OK until the car breaks down. Then I figure that they just don't make cars like they used to and get out and start walking.

If we all operated our cars the way we run our lives, the freeways and streets would be lined with abandoned vehicles. In general, we rely on our gauges to give us information to correctly operate our vehicles. Feelings are signals that provide us with information. We are not always sure what they mean, but we need to stop and find out what's happening. The issue is not whether they should or should not be there. They are there. They do exist. And I need to learn to pay attention to them. They tell me about me and what is going on within me. It is essential to our recovery for each of us to identify our feelings and experience them.

For example, let's say I suddenly recognize that I am feeling frustrated. Now at this point I haven't smashed any dishes, spoken harshly to anyone or even kicked the dog. So far, then, I have not done anything wrong or committed any sin. But I feel the pressure building inside. So, noticing this signal, I ask myself, "Why do I feel this way?"

As I reflect on my day I wonder if too much was going on at work. But no, things seem to be a little more stable than usual. Well, is it something with the family? Of course there are the typical hassles, but nothing out of the ordinary. Then I remember how irritated I was when I couldn't get the lawn mower started. A small thing, sure. But it just frustrated me so because I put a hundred dollars into fixing it last year and now it's broken again.

By noticing the signal and identifying its cause, I can then ask why this bugs me so. Maybe I feel cheated and need to talk to the repair shop. Maybe I feel like it's my fault the lawn mower is broken again. If I am responsible, I need to accept that and learn from it without condemning myself. If I am not responsible for it breaking, I need to accept that and learn not to blame myself for something that goes wrong that is not my fault.

These are all potentially constructive steps. Others are possible as well. They are much better than impulsively throwing the lawn mower away in disgust or misdirecting my anger to my family or coworkers because I failed to note the emotional signal and figure out what it meant. Toward the end of this chapter we'll look at some more emotional signals and what they might mean.

Feelings Are Physical

Painful memories that were repressed or blocked out can eventually lead to numerous physical complaints. Most of us have learned to label the symptoms as stress. I believe they represent an opportunity for healing the inner person. It is very common for ACAs to repress childhood memories due to trauma.

Physical responses are closely tied to our emotional responses. So much are the two connected that it is difficult to separate them. Many times the only place to start in recovery is body tension and physical signals of distress. Everyone carries the burdens of stress somewhere in their body. Perhaps the shoulders tighten up, lower back pain develops, gastro-intestinal disorders occur, headaches happen, allergies come or chronic pain becomes a daily dilemma. It may take some time for the body to break down, but eventually it does. Then we seek help to relieve the pain.

In my case I felt a tightening in my stomach. I slowly ruled out all of the foods that I was eating. My diet was bland, but I still felt stomach discomfort. Little did I know that the pain I felt was a signal of a greater discomfort. A pain that was deep inside of me that had been blocked for years. My body would not lie.

A person needs to see a physician and have the physical symptoms assessed and treated appropriately. However, I believe that many of the symptoms have their origin in the inadequate coping skills ACAs developed over the years. The symptoms need adequate medical treatments, but we need healing as well. The whole person needs treatment to develop a balanced life. Then the body will stop sending signals of distress.

In recovery, the body becomes an ally. We can use the signals our body gives as warning signals to pay attention to what's happening and what our responses can be in any given situation. Now when I sense tension in my stomach I am more alert to myself and the situation I'm in. I may not know exactly what is going on, but I trust something is happening either within me or within the situation I face.

I once worked with a person that was raised in an incestuous home and later married a battering husband. The only physical symptom she could identify was that her hands would ache, and she did not know why. Her feelings were blocked except for a chronic depression. But we trusted that her body was sending a distress signal and began to talk about the situations where her hands would bother her. We found that when her hands ached she was in a toxic, intrusive situation where she felt anxiety and out of control. Later, we made the connection between her hands aching and touching her father. It was such an intensely toxic incestuous relationship that her feelings and memories had to be blocked. But her body did not lie. From that start more feelings emerged, and the disowned child that had repressed years of trauma finally found love, acceptance and comfort.

We are whole people and the inner person desires healing, freedom and recovery. The body does not lie. Let us listen to its signals and appreciate the gift of pain our body sends to us.

5
THE VARIETY
OF FEELINGS

♦ ♦ ♦

I know I have a lot of feelings inside, but I can't let them out. It just feels like they will overwhelm me, and I will lose control. If I let them out I start to shake and have a pain build in my chest. *Fred*

When starting a recovery journey, we need to go slowly, develop awareness into the variety of feelings we have and learn to accept those feelings. When we use the AAA format (awareness, acceptance, action) we become more aware of what we feel which can make us more fearful. This is to be expected. For years we have not had permission to identify, experience or express our feelings. So to accept our feelings is a giant step to be sure.

Recovery is understanding and accepting where I have come from and where I now am. This frees me to move to where I want to be. As long as I refuse to acknowledge and accept where I am, I remain stuck. I'm never really free to move to the place of recovery I desire. It always remains beyond my grasp.

It is important during the early part of the healing journey to actively pursue strong supportive people that understand the growth process. We really do need each other for support, comfort, assurance and direction. It is also vital to reconnect with our spiritual side and look to God for the help and healing. This is the time to be carried by others and to look outside for the encouragement we need. We have just begun to learn to look within to take better care of ourselves. But the child within us does not have the confidence or experience to deal with the emerging awareness. We need to create as much safety as we can to allow the growth process to unfold. God in his wisdom sends the Spirit to walk with us, prompt us, comfort us, enable us and convict us as we journey toward healing.

Keeping this in mind, let's look then at some important emotions which cause adult children daily difficulty.

Abandonment

In many families a deep sense of abandonment arises within children. They develop a poor sense of belonging, and a fear of being left alone becomes a way of life. In many families of trauma, the homelife is fragile because it is characterized by people leaving or the threat of people leaving. Members of such families become preoccupied with living in a way that will prevent this from happening.

Often, children are confused by such chaos and draw erroneous conclusions about their feelings. They tend to blame themselves if someone leaves the family. They misinterpret messages intended to produce stability in the chaotic family. For instance, if children are told, "Be careful so you don't upset Mommy," they respond with guilt and fear. They will feel guilt if their parents get upset for any reason.

They will be afraid of saying or doing something that would upset their parents.

Either way children develop a sense of abandonment that later in adult relationships is characterized by a lack of trust and a belief that they cannot just be themselves. For if they do, other people will leave. Conflict in relationships becomes more difficult to endure because adult children no longer deal with the issue at hand but are overwhelmed by the deeper core issue of being abandoned.

Even in their spiritual lives, the fear of abandonment by God stymies their growth and development. Often, I hear believers struggle with not being able to trust God. It somehow does not feel right or appropriate for them. Trust is a fundamental feeling that families can help to produce or weaken.

Take time to read the account of Jesus' crucifixion in Matthew 27:45-50. The agony that he felt comes through. Christ wrestled with the feeling of abandonment. He asked why God was forsaking him. Even Christ could not escape such feelings. He knew his purpose and looked to the Father in prayer, but still dealt with the emotions the situation created. So we too will struggle with our deep feelings.

Feelings are signals, and the feeling of abandonment is a signal that provides information about ourselves and how we grew up. Even though God promises to never abandon us it will take some time before our old nature of fear is replaced with a new nature of trust. After gaining an awareness of where we are, we need comfort for the pain we feel and a program of transforming our perceptions about God's compassion for us (the topics of the next chapters).

Hurt

Chaos and trauma can mean many things to a child, especially hurt and pain. It is tough enough to be hurt, but the way the hurt is addressed in the family is important to understand. Let's address this feeling in three ways. First, the pain. Second, the person's unique reactions. Third, the way pain is handled in the family.

First, what is the pain they feel? Children of trauma suffer through tremendous amounts of abuse and neglect. This may come about through the use of drugs and alcohol. The abuse children suffer can be overt and obvious or covert and very subtle. One of my clients was punished by repeated whipping with a belt whenever he would drop his food while eating. Another was locked in her room for hours with the lights off and instructed to sit in the middle of the floor without moving because she had "upset" her mother. Another was sexually molested by her father, grandfather and uncle with admonitions by each to be quiet about it and tell no one or she would be punished. While these examples might be extreme, they are not uncommon.

More subtle ways of hurting children include being ridiculed for body characteristics or being called names such as "Beanpole," "Chicken Legs," "Fat Albert," "Four Eyes" and the like. It is hard to hear such things from other kids, but when it comes from the significant people in our family, the pain strikes deep. How many people remember bringing home a report card with A's and B's but being punished for that one C? Who has cleaned up their bedroom only to have someone point out the cobweb in the corner? It seemed like the focus was always on what was not done or not done good enough.

This hurt and pain is real. I believe the feelings of adults make perfect sense once the pain from childhood is understood. Traumatic homes create painful feelings.

Second, what are the unique reactions they have? Each person in the family is different. Some are more sensitive by nature than others, so they will experience hurtful situations with more internal pain. Some can disengage from their pain more easily than others. Some sense early that it does not feel good to be around particular people and so avoid them to cut down some of their pain. Still others gravitate toward a more pleasing style of behavior and thus cut down the pain. Others behave aggressively, releasing their hurt by hurting others.

Some become loners and isolate themselves in their own world of make-believe. They might become a great student and study to hide from the pain. Everyone is different and reacts to pain in many different manners.

Third, how do families in trauma handle pain? First, they stimulate it and then they block it. "You're just too sensitive." "You spend too much time in your room." "Why are you always so mopey?" Children are taught to not show their feelings or feel their feelings, and these patterns live on into adulthood.

Fear

Fear is the emotional response we have to threats or to something that is shocking and hard to understand. It alerts our system and heightens our attention. It is there to signal the need for protection. All children get frightened and are afraid. That is normal. In families where fear is understood, comfort and reassurance follows a child's fear. He or she needs the security and understanding of the adult to learn about fear and comfort.

In families of trauma, fears are stimulated, mismanaged and punished. In such families children fear abandonment, rejection, ridicule, criticism, abuse, neglect and non-acceptance. They are left unprotected. They receive no comfort. They are asked to deal with intense feelings that they are not emotionally equipped to cope with effectively. As adults the unresolved fears continue to terrorize them. It does not matter that they know they "shouldn't be afraid," they are. When a situation that is perceived as threatening comes to them, they will respond with fear. And later they become fearful of the fear they feel. That out-of-control, terror-filled, childlike sense revisits them time and time again.

Loss

There are many losses that every child has to face in childhood and later as an adult. I have reserved a chapter to more fully discuss the issues of loss and grief work (chapter seven). I believe it is essential for each person to identify and grieve the losses of childhood. Much of the healing work a person does in recovery is allowing the natural process of grief to heal the wounds of the hurt. One of my clients told me her recovery process was quite simple. She would move the feelings of mad to bad to sad and then would grieve the sadness. Over and over she was able to continue to heal the brokenness in her past by the concept of adequate grief work.

Shame

A core feeling most adult children have is a sense of shame. Often we speak of feeling guilty all of the time, but guilt and shame are not the same. Guilt is the feeling I have when I've done something wrong. Shame is the sense that I am wrong. Guilt is the feeling that comes after I've made a mistake. Shame is the feeling that I am a mistake. Families where trauma existed are primarily shame-based families. People in such a system have low self-worth and just feel bad. That feeling of badness is the feeling of shame.

If I make a mistake, I feel bad. This is shame. If I have fear, I feel bad. This is shame. If someone is upset with me, I feel bad. This is shame. If I did not do the job perfectly, I feel bad. This is shame. If I did not follow through on a decision I made, I feel bad. This is shame. If I'm saved but still feel lost, this is shame. If I cannot please God and others, I feel bad. This is shame. If I'm angry, I feel bad. This is shame. If I hurt someone else, I feel bad. This is shame. If I feel bad, I am bad. This is shame.

Shame directly influences self-worth. And the worth I feel about myself is characterized by shame. As we become aware of our feelings or enlightened about our destructive choices, shame usually follows.

Being raised in a shame-based family we learn to constantly rate ourself as either good or bad. Everything, including feelings, behavior, decisions, other's opinions, other family members' difficulties, are all used against our self-worth. Shame is the feeling that follows.

Adult children often find it difficult to accept that it is okay to have pain and hurt after becoming a believer. To admit to the brokenness inside evokes a sense of shame. It is like we are not as good as other believers. After all, the others do not look like they have pain. As one client told me, "I just feel different from the people at church. Why can't I be as happy as they are?"

As adult children we feel shame to have feelings of hurt and pain. We think that becoming a believer will make us happy, free of suffering and take away all brokenness. We think if we believe a little more, pray a better prayer, strengthen our faith, trust more, attend more services or involve ourselves in more activities, we would get rid of the feelings inside.

These messages mirror the same type of messages a shame-based family gives to children. If shame-based messages are given in a group or organization, the adult child easily believes them. Each of us likes to stay within our own comfort zone. To take a critical look at any system, especially the church, brings up feelings of disloyalty in us. This matches my feeling of disloyalty to my family when I talk about what really happened to me as a child. Disloyalty does not feel good, it feels bad, so I experience shame. This shame causes me to become stuck in my growth because I cannot talk about what's happening, cannot release the pain I feel and blame myself for having these feelings. So I try to pretend everything is OK.

To move from shame to self-respect is an important element of recovery. But the process of moving to self-respect is slow. For now we are just trying to identify core feelings. But it is essential, even in this early stage of awareness, to begin the healing and comforting process.

Take some time and pause. Recognize that you are not alone in feeling shame. Millions are experiencing shame at this moment. They

might not be able to identify it yet, but they are affected by it nonetheless. You are not alone. Your feelings reflect the journey you've
been on thus far in your life. And shame is no different. Be merciful
to yourself and give yourself permission to have the feelings you
discover. Shame is the cry of the person within us to alert us to the
need for comfort, gentleness and acceptance.

Anger

Anger is perhaps the most feared emotion we experience. This is
because of its intensity, its power to destroy and the admonitions we
learned against feeling any anger. Oftentimes, it is the emotion that
is most readily noticed by others. It empowers us to fight in situations
that are not just or right. It protects us from hurt and pain. It is used
to control others to make them be and do what we want. It also creates
pain and hurt in our lives and the lives of others. Often anger breeds
more anger in ourselves and others. It is feared because it, more than
any other emotion, characterizes being out of control. People become
unpredictable and chaotic when they are angry. This scares us. Let's
see if we can make some sense out of this emotion.

Following our model that feelings are signals, what does anger
mean to us? First, in situations where our self-esteem is attacked, it is
normal to feel anger. Adult children raised in shame-based families
have their self-respect attacked a great deal. As a result they often feel
very angry.

Second, in situations where true injustice and human violation occurs, anger is normal. Children raised in the trauma of abuse and
neglect will rightly experience this feeling.

Third, any situation where the value of life is denigrated evokes
anger. Watching our neighbors, friends and family ruined by the
greed and insensitivity of others brings it forth.

Fourth, anger is present when things do not go according to our
own plans and standards. We do not have to have a traumatic back-

ground to experience anger when a "crazy" driver cuts us off in the road.

Fifth, any time our tender feelings are stirred up, anger steps forward to protect us and attempts to control the situation. By tender feelings I mean our fears, inadequacies, insecurities and feelings of insignificance.

Our difficulty with anger is similar to the other emotions—we never learned what to do with it in a constructive manner. Formerly, our recourse was either to express it and become aggressive or to push it down and become passive. Often what was modeled for us in the family becomes our style too. Also, most of us relate anger to the behavior we witnessed when someone was angry. We equate anger with yelling, hitting, criticizing and withdrawing. Ephesians 4:26-27 says, " 'In your anger do not sin.' Do not let the sun go down while you are still angry, and do not give the devil a foothold." How do we learn to deal with anger in this way?

Learning the skills needed to cope with this powerful emotion is what recovery is about. It is no different from learning how to deal with the other emotions. Using the AAA recovery format we are building awareness in this chapter so some insights to coping with anger will follow in later chapters. For now it is important to take a realistic look at ourselves. Am I angry? When do I get angry? What situations are most difficult for me? Whom do I express the most anger toward? What do I normally do when I feel angry? Do I have difficulty identifying my anger?

I used to call my anger everything but anger. I would say "I'm *very* frustrated," "*extremely* annoyed" and "*highly* irritated." To call what I was feeling anger brought forth shame and self-condemnation. It would make me just like the angry people I could not stand. If I was angry like them, then I was no better than them. And I did not like them. So how could I like myself? I needed to break through my denial and learn to identify what was really happening within me. I was angry. But I was more than just angry. I was scared, insecure, inadequate and felt insignificant. Anger was the protecting emotion.

Anger, however, was not acceptable to me, so I was caught in a dilemma. To express what I truly felt was shameful. To push it down and pretend it did not exist left me stuck and feeling bad. So I used denial for years. I would block it out and call the response something else. But this does not work very well as an adult. I would still experience intense emotions and deny they existed. I needed to learn that anger is a part of being a human and a reflection of my journey. I concluded that if Jesus could be angry and experience the emotion I dreaded so much, then maybe I could allow myself some anger also.

The questions I asked earlier may help you gain awareness and insight into your anger. I found it helpful to acknowledge my anger by saying, "I am a person who is experiencing some anger right now. I am not an angry person. I'm just feeling anger now. I feel many things—joy, sadness, fear. And right now I feel angry." I would attempt to accept myself even if I did not know why I felt what I did. I was willing to let anger become a signal to help me understand what I was experiencing about life at that time. I would then try to dig deeper for the tender emotions that were the source of my anger. I usually found those and many other tender emotions which were in need of comfort, understanding and gentleness.

Sometimes, it was important for me to walk away from a situation that made me angry. In that way I would gather myself and my thoughts, and then use the AAA format. The time can also be used to comfort and soothe myself. It is also a time where I would develop a new plan for what I was going to do as I walked back into the situation. Since we all are creatures of habit and react in patterns, the need to break the pattern is vital. Somehow, we have got to interrupt the way we normally react.

I also found the break a good time to write. I would ask some basic questions and record what I could about myself. I would ask what happened? How am I feeling? What did I do? What am I thinking about? How am I viewing this situation? What do I want to do? Each of the answers would bring greater clarity about myself and the reactions that I experienced.

Live or Memorex?

Television advertising for Memorex audiotapes shows a performer singing and breaking a glass. Then music breaks a glass again, only this time we are asked, "Is it live or is it Memorex?" But the result is the same, the glass breaks. This impresses me, not because it is an outstanding television commercial, but because this is what happens to ACAs. We never know if it is "live or Memorex." That is, we never know whether what we are experiencing is really the result of what is happening today or whether it is our emotional tapes playing from the past.

Let me give some examples. Virginia feels terrified when her husband, Bruce, leaves for his business trip. Is this a reaction that has roots in her childhood when she was constantly abandoned and left alone?

Or Tom, forty-five, owns his own business but telephones to talk with his dad about every business decision. He is afraid to make a mistake and risk going against Dad's opinions. Can it be that Tom is still searching for the approval from his dad which he did not receive in childhood?

Ruth, a divorced mother of three, returns to college but feels guilty and full of shame and unworthiness because she is spending money on herself to pursue her education. Can it be that old tapes are playing, saying she does not deserve anything good for herself?

Recovery means turning off the tapes that continue to shatter our experiences today. It means learning the distinction between the Memorex tapes of the past and the person I am today. Recovery means that the power of the old life no longer becomes the only influence over the feelings and choices we make today. It means I can create new and more effective tapes. These are new ways of responding to my present and my future. Before recovery if a situation arose that was similar to one from my youth, I would probably respond with the old tapes. This is normal. In time, as recovery emerges, I can develop other tapes that will produce more constructive and healthy responses. But I will be prone to the old response for a long time.

Recovery is a slow and gentle process that affords us the opportunity to heal the memories, the hurts and pains, the destructive choices and the injustice of our past. But situations like those of our childhood trauma will exist as a tender spot for years in our adult life. We never outgrow our need for comfort and healing. However, the pains will lessen, the intensity will diminish, and the duration of the pain is shorter.

In capturing what we feel, understanding the feelings, accepting the feelings and comforting the inner person, we set the stage for recovery to unlock our real person. A vital part of this recovery is learning to let go of the power the past holds over us. However, the power memories exert on us can cause us to reopen old wounds. These drive us to attack, avoid or escape instead of facing the hurt, dealing with it and moving on.

6
HEALING EMOTIONS: THE NEED FOR A COMFORTER

♦ ♦ ♦

I'm so tired of being angry at myself. It seems everything I feel is not okay. What I want isn't okay. The truth is I'm not okay. Mom was right. I should have been just like my sister. I try harder to stop the feelings, but nothing seems to help. Mainly, now I try to avoid my family. *Jan, forty-year-old ACA*

The LORD comforts his people and will have compassion on his afflicted ones. *Isaiah 49:13*

I have set the LORD always before me. Because he is at my right hand, I will not be shaken. Therefore my heart is glad and my tongue rejoices; my body also will rest secure, because you will not abandon me to the grave. *Psalm 16:8-10*

Be my rock of refuge, to which I can always go. *Psalm 71:3*

If healing is to happen within us, the pain and trauma of our life need to be faced. This puts us in a very vulnerable state. We become more aware of the pain, yet we do not know what to do with that pain.

As children we desperately needed comfort, acceptance, love and validation. If we had received these key ingredients as we grew up, healing would have taken place very naturally. But we didn't. So now as adults, we need to learn how to comfort ourselves when we face our pain and brokenness. This begins the natural process of healing.

What Comfort Is Not

Often we hear that acceptance and comfort promote inappropriate behavior. This sounds like a nice way to excuse a person from taking responsibility for oneself. Acceptance is honestly looking at ourself, learning from our failures and mistakes, and seeking to break our old patterns of behavior. Comfort is the validation of ourself as a person, not of our behavior. It is restoring our worth and dignity. It is not an excuse to sin.

Furthermore, comfort is not a chance to say "poor me." Having a pity-party does not increase self-worth. "Poor me" is a childish attempt at self-comfort, but instead of creating forgiveness it creates more anger. So we remain stuck and hopeless to make a change.

As we move ahead in the recovery process, we stop diminishing the significance of our problems. This leads to an increased awareness of the emotional damage we are carrying from our family. But at this point in recovery we really do not know the options available to solve our problems. So our goal becomes to validate and accept the pain.

In laying a foundation supporting the need for acceptance and comfort in our recovery process, consider the basic needs of children. Glenn says in his book *Raising Children for Success* that he considers all children to be high-risk individuals. Further, he says that skills need to be developed and maintained over a lifetime in order to become low risk and highly successful. These skills deal primarily with the child's perception of self-significance, capability and emotions. The family model becomes the style the children use as adults.

Laura's Story

Laura came to counseling because she felt fearful and out of control. Neither parent was alcoholic. In fact, both were strict fundamentalist Christians. The atmosphere in the home was rigid, overcontrolled, serious and punitive. Discipline was handed out severely for any action that was not "right." She recalls receiving a harsh spanking for talking too long after church with her best friend. "When the family is ready to go, everyone should be in the car at the same time," her dad had said. She felt bad and was terrified on the ride home from church because dad had told her, "We'll take care of you when we get home." The twenty-minute drive lasted for hours.

Today she says, "I feel out of control. Nothing I can do will ever change anything. I just sit and shake sometimes. It's so stupid. I'm an adult and a Christian and there is no reason why I need to be afraid. My family would be better off if I just left. I try to be a loving mother. My husband just yells at me to stand up for myself. But I can't and I should be able to. God and I haven't had much of a relationship for years. And I feel bad about that."

Do you hear in Laura's words how basic skills were not developed from her family? Laura did not know that the manner in which she treated herself reflected the treatment given to her as a child. This is because, as someone once said, "the perceptions we hold about ourselves mirror our family systems."

The Basic Needs of Children

There are many basic ingredients that promote healthy and mature development. The following is a summary of material from several authors (Glenn, 1987; Larsen, 1988; Middleton-Moz, 1989; Erickson, 1963):

☐ A sense of *trust:* people are safe, touch is safe and people will not neglect and abuse me. I am protected.

☐ A sense of *belonging:* people will not abandon me, I am a part of something bigger than me, and I am included just because I'm me.

☐ A sense of *capability:* I can explore and create, I can make an impact on my world, I can take care of myself. I can accomplish tasks.

☐ A sense of *value and worth:* I am valued for just being me. I am unique and that is OK. I am different from others in the family and that is not bad.

☐ A sense of *love:* this place is nonviolent. I feel compassion and gentleness from those around me.

☐ A sense of *healthy consistency and predictability:* my family is not organized around chaos and unpredictability. It is a place I can count on for safety. I learn to count on the family routine and rituals to provide structure. Rules are fair and promote each person's uniqueness. Rules do not keep changing.

☐ A sense of *boundaries:* each person has access to the others in the family but respect for ourselves and others is held as a high value. Intrusions are few and dealt with by openness. Isolation is rare because others notice the withdrawing and are willing to talk about it.

☐ A sense of *spirituality:* there is a bigger reason for living that ties the family together. The child needs to have morals shaped and an understanding of a larger plan for life. We are purposeful beings, and children need to experience a healthy sense of spirituality in the family.

The keys to establishing these areas rest in the family dynamic, parental modeling and personalities of the children. Parents need to create an atmosphere of safety, nurturing and comfort. But they need to present firm, yet loving, boundaries and rules for living that are grounded in reality. Dysfunctional parents recreate the chaos and trauma they experienced as children. Their only clear model for raising a family is the family in which they were raised. So their children come along and another generation is affected with the same worn-out, ineffective and dysfunctional patterns. Pain is handed down from generation to generation.

In early recovery we need to re-establish the areas that were missing, skipped or damaged in our family of origin. As adults in recovery we need to establish the concept of acceptance and comfort on a conscious level. We are dealing with a child within us that is still wounded from childhood. That wounding will never go away until a sufficient amount of comfort and acceptance is developed to free us from the past.

Brandon's Story

Brandon spent most of the counseling session angry at himself for making a mistake at work. He felt stupid and questioned whether he would ever be a person capable of doing anything correct. He said, "I knew better than to drive my machinery over the bank, but I thought I could make it. Well, the boss was yelling at me and all the men looked at me like I didn't have a brain in my head. The fact that I hurt my shoulder in the accident is the payment I got. That is just what I deserved. I'm thinking about quitting, but I don't know what to do as a career. My wife is real scared because I've left other jobs and this has been the best job I've ever had. But I just don't know if I can face them all at work after the arm is feeling better and the doctor releases me."

We discussed his ideas about making mistakes and the deeper feelings he held about himself. He began to tell a story that stood out in his mind from his childhood.

"One time I was riding my bike on some paths behind our house. I was getting real good at some of the jumps. A lot of the kids would follow me and try to do the jump the way I did. But I fell one afternoon and cut my knee and hands pretty bad. Dad heard me crying and came out to the paths. He was real mad at me. He was yelling at me. He told me to stop crying and quit acting like a child. 'You won't die from a little cut,' he said. He was going to spank me for not being more careful. He told me that this is just what you get when you don't pay attention. My father laughed and then looked at the other boys and said, 'Pretty good leader you guys are following. He doesn't look so cocky now does he?' "

Brandon sobbed as he held his head in his hands. He continued, "I stopped riding on the paths and took up baseball. But secretly I always wanted to go back and show the other kids I was better than them. But I never did. You know this may sound silly but I've watched these stunt riders on TV. You know the ones on the BMX bikes. I hurt inside every time and do not let my son watch it. I tell him it's silly and stupid. But I'm really envious of those bike riders. Somebody let them ride on a path somewhere."

I asked him what he thought the little boy needed the most after the accident. Brandon responded quickly with anger, "I did not need to be called stupid and made fun of in front of my friends. And I did not need him to laugh at me and yell at me and punish me." I asked him again if he could identify what the little boy needed the most. He was quiet and then replied, "I've never thought about it. I just get angry." We decided to let him think about it over the week and try to conceptualize what he needed.

The next session Brandon returned with some writing from his journal about the accident. Several pages were written without much insight. But later in the week the writing changed. He showed me what he wrote.

"Bran wanted someone to care. I wanted Dad to hold me and tell me everything was OK. I wanted him to fix my cuts because I really thought I would bleed too much and die. I wanted him to be proud of me and let me go back to the path. I wanted him to tell the other boys that it is OK to cry because I already felt embarrassed because they were watching me. I wanted him to let me know it was OK to fall down and he would not pull away from me and ever hurt me. I guess this is what I wanted. Sounds pretty silly, doesn't it?"

Later Brandon would see that the needs he had as a child were still waiting to be affirmed. He would also understand that the way his father treated him was the way he treated himself. So when he would make a mistake, his automatic style was to make fun of himself and become very self-critical. This would lead to increased bad feelings, and then he would want to run away. Brandon began to see the themes from childhood continuing to play out over and over in his adult life. Only now the person doing the parenting was himself.

Looking back at the construction accident he was able to determine that the greater pain he felt had little to do with the actual behavior of driving his machine over the bank. The pain was a re-enactment of the shame he has always had from his childhood. His wounded heart was still wanting the other "big people" in his life to not embarrass him publicly but to accept him as a person who makes mistakes yet is not bad.

Brandon knew running away was not his best choice, but he did not know what to do with the hurt inside. He began to believe that a significant price of his recovery work had to do with his own acceptance of himself. This was true in spite of the shouting in his head that said, "You really do not need this acceptance stuff. You just need to do it better. You should not have made the mistake and you should not be in this mess."

I began by helping Brandon identify the feelings he experienced. Feelings like hurt, shame, guilt, fear and inadequacy. Next Brandon had to externalize those feelings. So he wrote about them in his daily journal, and he began to talk with his wife about his fears and feelings. I coached her to understand the difference between Brandon talking about his feelings and the decision he would eventually make about the job. She too had fears. She did not want him to talk because it used to always precede quitting his job.

As Brandon would talk, his wife would listen, be supportive, accept his pain and wounded spirit. Brandon would ask for what he wanted each day. Sometimes he needed to be held or just have her listen. Other times he needed her to tell him he was important to her, his family appreciated him, she respected him, loved him and believed in him.

Brandon found ways to be gentle with himself. He started taking his breaks at work and used the time to read, go for a walk or listen to music. He would begin to give himself permission to feel and accept his feelings as part of being a human. He learned to appreciate his feelings. He worked to fight the urge to disconnect himself from what he felt. At first, he did not feel a lot different. But he did confess that he felt better for a little time. The need for comfort and acceptance of himself, his feelings and his needs was new and unfamiliar to Brandon. But it seemed the only alternative left to deal with the pain in his heart.

"Nothing else has worked. So I'll keep trying," Brandon said. Weeks passed and the struggle to run away became less, the hurts reduced and the bad days became fewer. There were longer periods of good feelings about himself, in between the dark days.

As Brandon's acceptance of himself grew, he was more honest with himself about his emotions and the critical attitude he held about himself and his family. The compassion he was providing for himself was spilling over into his family. He cried in front of the kids for the first time and explained to them what it meant to be sad. He was sorry for hurting them with his harsh words. The children cried. They talked about how sad and scared they felt. This was hard for Brandon, but he continued to accept and comfort himself as he became more aware of the pain within himself and the pain his harshness had brought to his family.

Months have passed since I first met Brandon. Healing takes time but it is accomplished one day at a time. Brandon is now committed to his recovery path. He has extended his support network to an ACA group and a men's fellowship group. The issues Brandon struggled to overcome have repeated over and over as he faces life. Some are not dealt with in their entirety, but in time I'm convinced he will work them through. He has greatly reduced his most destructive patterns, especially those that perpetuated the damage to his self-worth and the destruction of his family. He is still working at the same job and is almost debt-free. He is planning his family's first vacation. He lives with greater balance and self-responsibility.

One day Brandon came into the office with a paper rolled up in his hand. With a gleam in his eye and a boyish shyness, he said, "You'll never believe what I did. No, you probably will." He unfolded the paper. It was a page torn out of a Sears catalog. On it were mountain bikes that were circled and figures scratched out on the side of the page.

"After the last session I went and ordered them. I took them home Friday after work. I spent most of the evening putting them together. When everyone got up, we went riding on Saturday. I was so happy. As the wind blew into my face, I felt free. My son went off the road and over a small mound of dirt and yelled, 'Dad, look at me. Ain't I great?' I replied, 'You sure are great.' A tear came to my eye as I yelled to him, 'And if you ever fall just call me and I'll be there . . . I'll be there.' "

Brandon could offer to his son a gift he did not receive as a boy. But it was a gift he was learning to give to himself. The more he accepted, nurtured and comforted himself, the wounds slowly healed. The greatest gift we give to our family is our own recovery and healing. We become more able to see the pain in others and comfort them.

As our wounded memories, feelings and inner self are soothed, our heart flows with compassion and love for others with wounded hearts. It is like a recycling process. I love because I've been loved. I comfort because I've been comforted. I forgive as I've been forgiven.

As adult children raised in dysfunctional homes, we develop behaviors that are intended to be self-comforting but turn out to be compulsive and destructive to ourselves and others. So we never really meet the inner needs we have. But as we heal our emotional past, we become able to see our present situations more clearly and act with greater creativity to address them.

Comforting Strategies

There are a number of comforting strategies that many in recovery have found helpful. With yourself:

1. Learn to change the rules about how feelings are identified and expressed, and the meaning feelings carry.

☐ Give permission to feel what I do feel instead of what I should feel.

☐ Own the feelings as a part of me and my journey.

☐ Embrace the feelings as a part of me.

☐ Give permission to express feelings directly.

2. Learn to take action that nurtures one's self.

☐ Write or read poetry.

☐ Listen to soothing music.

☐ Go for walks.

☐ Take a child with you on a walk, and learn from their point of view of the world.

☐ Take a long bath with bubbles or oil.

☐ Give yourself flowers, cards or a night out.

☐ Pick up a hobby you once had but have left behind.

☐ Develop a new hobby that has interested you.

☐ Have a party. Invite a favorite friend.

☐ Plan some play activities. That's right, *plan* to have some fun.

☐ Take up fishing, golfing, handball (my favorite), painting or whatever.

☐ Learn to take breaks throughout your day.

☐ Start writing a journal.

☐ Pray or meditate.

☐ Find an animal to be your pet.

3. Develop safe and comforting visualizations.

☐ Remember a place or event in your past that was safe, fun and comforting. It might be a friend's house, grandma or a favorite childhood toy, or an accomplishment that brings up good feelings. Practice remembering these.

☐ Invent new ones where none exist.

☐ Focus on scenes where God or Christ is holding you close. Where he is loving you. If that is too hard, try to let him hold you as a child. Sometimes it helps to have a picture of yourself as a child and focus on the picture while adding Christ to the scene.

4. Develop rituals that are care-giving to yourself.

☐ Take breaks at work or times in the evening to reflect on the day or a morning time to focus on the day.

5. Develop affirmations for yourself.

☐ Write out a list that can be read often throughout a day or used during the breaks mentioned above.

6. Learn to develop a patience for your healing work. It will take some time to grow into a new comfort zone of acceptance and comfort.

With others:

1. Develop a network of people you can trust. Seek out fellowship.

☐ Attend group therapy, 12-step meetings or a church fellowship.

☐ Develop a new family of choice that is different from your family of origin. Start with one person and then add another.

☐ Develop a phone list of persons you trust and use it.

2. Break the rule of not asking for what you want.

☐ Learn to frame your requests for soothing and comfort clearly and directly.

3. Go to the most significant person in your life and ask for comfort. It will probably stretch the person you ask, but you both will start getting healed in the process.

☐ If the significant person cannot or is unable to help, rely upon the others in your network.

4. Find a person you can confide in honestly. This will help your journey with accountability.

5. Seek out group therapy or a therapist that is familiar with the issues facing you in recovery.

With God:

1. Develop an honesty with God. Tell him as much as you can. All of your awareness of your feelings, thoughts and actions need to be brought before him.

2. Meditate often on his love, acceptance and comfort.

☐ Read and take time to dwell at leisure on such passages from the Bible as Psalm 145; Romans 8:31-39 and Luke 15:11-31 (thinking of God as the father of the prodigal son).

3. Invite him into all the parts of your heart, mind, feelings and actions.

4. Ask for his Spirit to comfort, lead and direct your path.

5. Admit your need daily for his power in your life.

6. Read his Word to gain understanding about his comfort, truth, love and hope.

7. Seek fellowship with others who teach a balance of truth, acceptance and healing.

May your journey be one that is filled with comfort as you look at your pain. I would like to close this chapter with one of my favorite Bible passages.

"I waited patiently for the LORD; he turned to me and heard my cry. He lifted me out of the slimy pit, out of the mud and mire; he set my feet on a rock and gave me a firm place to stand" (Psalm 40:1-2).

7
HEALING
EMOTIONS: GRIEF

♦ ♦ ♦

*I*s it normal for a person to cry as much as I am? It seems the tears just flow for the slightest reason. Watching a TV show, seeing a mother and child together, hearing a sad song and having a friend just notice me all send me crying. Am I normal? Or am I crazy? Why won't I just grow up and stop all of this constant crying? *Mandy*

---

*W*hen does the pain stop? Will I ever be able to not hurt on the inside as much as I do now? I heard someone say at a meeting the other night to trust the process. But I'm tired of this hurt. I didn't used to feel this much pain. If this is recovery, it stinks. *Robert*

The LORD is close to the brokenhearted and saves those who are crushed in spirit. *Psalm 34:18*

For many, there is an incredible sadness within us, a sadness buried for years as denial blocked the reality of our pain. To grieve means facing the losses we have encountered throughout life, and feeling the pain of those losses. It means adjusting who we are as a result of facing those losses, and reinvesting ourselves in the world today with a new sense of meaning.

Much of the process of grieving is similar to other recovery work. We follow the AAA format of building awareness, then acceptance and comfort, and finally moving beyond the losses with appropriate action steps. We will first look at why we have difficulty grieving and then present the stages of appropriate grief work.

Blocks to the Grief Process

John James and Frank Cherry, in their book *The Grief Recovery Handbook,* listed some myths about grief which we learned in our childhood.

1. Bury Your Feelings. Many times the idea of denying our feelings starts with the message we get from our parents over small losses. I remember one client who discussed his first loss. He was seven and left his favorite toy outside. When he went out the next morning, it was gone. He cried and "carried on" for a couple of days until his dad told him to not make a big deal about losing the toy. He wanted his father's approval, so he stuffed the sad feelings and pretended that losing his favorite toy was no big deal. Inside he hurt, but he could not let anyone know.

2. Replace the Loss. This same client was told that a new toy would be purchased next week. While that was nice, the new toy was not the same as the old favorite one. But he could not show how he felt. He was told to appreciate how much the parent loved him for getting a new replacement toy. If the boy had sad feelings about losing the old toy, he felt bad.

3. Grieve Alone. When this boy looked sad, he was told to go to his room until he could straighten up and be happy. The parents did not deal with their own grief, so how could they handle the grief of the little boy? Children learn fast. Soon he would just leave whenever he did not feel good.

4. Regret the Past. If we cannot face the loss and resolve the feelings we seem to continually look backward and wish for things to be different. We spend more and more time creating a myth of what should have been rather than what really was. We are prone to feel guilty and angry at ourselves for the choices we made. Also, we resent the choices others made that harmed us.

5. Do Not Trust. Pain that comes to us in the form of loss often stays unresolved. So we learned to cut down the potential for pain. This is why we do not attach ourselves to anyone deeply. We cannot trust they will not leave or hurt us so we do not risk getting close. We attach to things and not people. We think that people will leave, and it's hard to replace them, but we can always buy a new car or a different piece of furniture.

These blocks to grief are become our "truth" about loss. It is only because the pain within becomes too great that we have to face ourselves. For some the pain is a steady growth over the years, for others a major crisis disrupts the denial and stuffing processing and leaves our raw emotions exposed.

Most of us spend a great deal of energy avoiding our losses. While avoidance does bring a temporary relief, the long-term consequences will always be more pain and more losses to face. Some of us will choose a compulsive behavior such as alcohol, drugs, eating, sex, work or religious fanaticism to keep away the pain within us.

Exercises for Grief Work
Each of us face crisis and have pain. It does not matter what crisis you are now facing. If you have pain, you have loss. And you learned how you are supposed to deal with the loss. Perhaps it is not working. The

rest of the chapter will focus on facilitating appropriate grief work in each of us.

Since many of us do not recognize losses, let me list some of them to help us identify where we may have never grieved.

1. Important Person—death, separation, divorce, rejection, illness, children leaving.

2. Physical Loss—part of one's body, an accident, an image of body which does not match cultural expectations, self-esteem, sexual or physical abuse.

3. Childhood—not having healthy parents, loss of early objects of attachment (toys, pet), low status in the family, separation, divorce, chaos, trauma.

4. Adult Loss—jobs, relationships, dreams or goals, health, transitions, mistakes, victimized by burglary, assault.

5. Material Loss—objects of value, money, property, sentimental object and collections.

Identifying Your Losses. An exercise that I have used with many clients is a loss-history diary. This does not have to be formal and superpsychological to produce a wealth of information about oneself and one's attitudes. One does not need to get everything "right" on the graph. Just start. Some will not want to do the exercise but prefer to simply identify losses by listing those that come to mind separately. I'll look at that method later.

These are simple instructions for a loss-history diary.

1. Write your date of birth on the top of the page.

2. Draw a line across the top of a sheet of paper and divide it in ten-year sections:

10	20	30	40	50

3. Begin the loss graph with the earliest loss that you can remember and mark it on the graph. For example, you can see how

Joe's chart looked in figure 1.

Joe   born December 5, 1950

        10   20   30   40

   57   dog

   59 bike

          64 B.B. team

            67 dropped out H.S.

                 73 grandfather

                      79 divorce

                           83-87 over-
                                drinking

                                 89 DWI

Figure 1. *Joe's Loss-History Diary*

4. Describe briefly each entry. For Joe it looked like this:

57—dog. I lost my puppy.

59—bike. My bike was stolen while I was at the park.

64—B.B. team. I was cut from the basketball team, but all my friends made it.

67—High school. I dropped out of high school and never got my diploma.

73—My grandfather died. He was real special to me.

81—Divorce. I was divorced by my wife. She left me and said I was a lousy husband.

83-87—Drinking. I lost a lot of jobs and was drinking a lot. I do not remember much about that time period.

89—DWI. I was arrested for drinking and driving, and my world just seemed to collapse.

5. Go back over the losses and write out what you felt about yourself at the time and how you were taught to deal with the loss.

Joe, like many of us, learned to bury his feelings. He pretended his losses did not matter, did not talk about them, blamed other people and did whatever he wanted to do with no regard for other's feelings because he believed they did not care about him.

6. Tell someone you trust everything you can about the losses you have faced, the feelings that have surfaced and the rules you learned to cope with loss.

If you are facing a loss that is current and you do not want to go through the history, then just write as much as you can about the current loss, the feelings you have, the meaning the loss has for you and the way you have been handling the loss up to this point. Then share that with your support person or group.

The important thing is that you recognize the losses, the feelings that are attached to them, and the style you use to cope with the losses. By writing and talking about them, you are breaking the style of not talking, not feeling and avoiding the pain. In the AAA format, this is building awareness.

Writing in a Journal. Another exercise is journaling. Here is one example of a part of a journal a client was using to build awareness each week.

I was listening to a tape about abandonment from a workshop I recently attended. I was trying to get some ideas that I might use in my practice [as a therapist]. As I listened to the tape I became aware that I was feeling really weird. I just told myself that I was tired and it had been a long conference so that would explain why I felt weird. But the feelings grew. I decided I had enough of the tape so I turned it off. But the feelings grew. I thought that this is really stupid. After all I'm a therapist and I was trying to improve my skills with my clients. But the feelings grew. I stopped and tried to identify what I felt. And then it hit me, I feel abandoned. But why? (We therapists love to analyze the reasons feelings exist but fail to follow our own suggestions of acceptance.) I could not find an answer. My husband has not left me. My job is okay. My kids are doing okay in school. Why the feelings?

She brought me the journal entry, and we went over it together. As she read it out loud and gave herself permission to feel the feeling of abandonment, she began to cry.

We discovered that in the previous few weeks she had several patients in her practice leave without notice. They did not show up for the next session scheduled. And some did not want to come back at all. Others said they would think about returning but not now. With each person leaving she would justify intellectually, "They needed to do that for themselves." But she never got in touch with the sense she felt of being abandoned.

This was just like her childhood. She was the primary caregiver in her family. She was the oldest of four children. The parents would leave, and no one would talk about what was going on. Dad would split and Mom would follow. She was told to keep things together. She spent days and years pushing down the feelings of being left and needing to be strong so she could take care of the rest of the family. She could not talk about what she felt. What she needed did not matter. Others were depending on her to not break under the tension. Today, as a therapist, the scene is the same. She discounts feelings of abandonment in order to be strong for her clients.

Over time she continued to write in journal form whenever sadness, loss and abandonment would come up. Each time she would feel the sadness, share the feelings and comfort herself. As the unfinished childhood loss of her parents slowly healed, she found herself less confused with her clients, more willing to discuss the client issues around abandonment, and developed more clarity about her role as a therapist. She had a better sense within the counseling relationship of the work the client needed to do and the work she needed to do.

I share this example as another type of writing that many find helpful. The main points are to write, feel the feelings, share the story and find ways to help the healing process. For some talking is a primary mode. Such a person should attend the meetings or sessions you need in order to talk about the pain. Whatever works, just risk breaking the silence that denial has created within us.

Sharing Our Losses. After we begin to identify our losses and the feelings we have, it is essential to talk with others and experience the feelings we have. In this stage, we can gain a sense of comfort and acceptance. By telling our story we begin to diminish the power the emotional pain has held over us for years. We find we are not alone, others share in our pain and we begin to break down the isolation that we have felt for years. Some of the craziness we feel goes away simply because we make valid what we experienced growing up. For most ACAs there is a deep fear we will go crazy or out of control if we face our pain. That simply is not true.

If the pain seems too intense to look at with the support person you have chosen, seek professional help. Each of us need guides to help us on the journey. Do not hesitate to find someone qualified in the recovery process to assist you if your current support person or group is not able to provide the needed help.

Early Grief Process

Up to this point the work of identifying losses, feeling the feelings, sharing our grief and learning to comfort are all part of the early grief work. I believe most adult children from dysfunctional homes suffer delayed grief reactions. So it makes sense that the recovery work we do will have a lot of grief work within it.

During early grief work, most of us struggle to find a purpose for what happened. Life does not seem fair. It is grossly unjust. We cannot find any sane reason for the loss we are feeling. The more intense or significant the loss, the less it makes sense. "It just does not seem right." Over the time we are grieving, our perspective begins to

change slightly. We start asking questions that seek to find meaning
in the losses. Our primary response to loss is denial. In order to find
new meaning in the losses, we need to continue to face the losses,
share the pain and allow the healing of our mind and emotions to
take place.

Following our AAA model of awareness, acceptance and action, I
refer you to the previous chapter for tips on creating as much comfort
as you can while you grieve your losses. Grieving does not have to be
a time of trauma if we take steps to comfort, share and develop safety
when we hurt. During our grief work it is normal to feel helpless, have
mood swings, confusion, anger, guilt and depression. We need to
structure an environment around us that supports us as much as
possible. This is a time of reaching out and relying on others and God
to provide the comfort we need as we face ourselves honestly and take
responsibility for our grief work.

As we have worked through our major losses, we will be able to help
others in their early grief work. Grief work is where we weep along
with others in pain and rejoice with the victories. As we heal our losses
we are in a position to help others.

Bringing Closure to Our Losses

I believe that by following the structures that I've presented, healing
will begin to take place. But sometimes it seems like the loss never
comes to an end. I do not believe we ever forget the loss, but the
intensity of the pain is greatly decreased. We are left with tender spots
on our hearts from the childhood wounds. Many of us need to continue with the AAA format and take more action steps to bring completion.

Some of the most creative ideas for dealing with loss come from this
final stage of recovery work. This is a hard stage to enter too early.
But when one has worked through much of the pain, this stage brings
more completion to the loss we are facing. It seems this stage is like

a final letting go and moving beyond the loss. All of the small shifts in our perspective prepare us for this stage. Because our view of life slowly changes to incorporate the loss, we are moved gently to decide what we need to have happen here.

You decide when it is best in your recovery path to incorporate the following steps. James and Cherry call these areas recovery communications. The three areas are making amends, offering forgiveness and expressing significant emotional statements.

Making Amends. Many times we have regrets. Given the history of abuse and trauma many of us faced as children, it may seem strange that I would talk about making amends. But I believe we, in some way, continue the violence and insanity of our childhood.

Some of us may have treated our family with the same violence that was given to us. Others have continued to hurt those close to them long into adulthood. Sometimes, we knew we needed to talk about the craziness in our family but we kept silent. No matter what the behavior, we too are fused in some way to the abuse and need to take responsibility for our reaction to it.

One of my clients named Fred had spent considerable time in his recovery work. He was involved in individual therapy and a support group. He had processed a lot of grief work from his violent childhood. After a group session where he listened to another participant talk about being responsible for keeping distance from his father, Fred realized that he too had spent years keeping his father away from him. He understood his behavior was motivated by the need for protection. But he more deeply understood that a part of his motivation was punishment for his father. He took every opportunity to hurt his father, insult him and put him down.

Fred eventually gained an insight that was very painful to face. He saw that he was no different from his father. Their behavior was different, but the result was the same. He was hurting another person. He resolved to clear the air with his father. After arranging a meeting, he sat down and briefly apologized for his actions and asked for forgiveness from his father. Fred was finally feeling a sense of freedom from the attachment with his dad. Their relationship improved a little, but Fred's sense of growth and healing soared.

Offering Forgiveness. Often we think we have forgiven someone, but we have never made the act of forgiveness real. Let me explain. One of the reasons healing does not fully take place is that we have the tendency to intellectualize the process. That is, we think to ourselves what we need to do (forgive them), and because we thought about it, we think it is done. But we need to follow the AAA format and make the idea real through action.

I remember listening to a client talk about all the work she had done releasing her mother and facing her losses. But she still felt stuck. She said, "I've forgiven my mom but do not have any good feelings about her." I asked her if she had told her mom. She quickly responded, "No way."

Until we actually verbalize in some way our forgiveness, we cannot experience the release we need. Forgiving people means no longer viewing them through the eyes of the offense. We do not minimize what was done, but we develop a broader vision of the acts done to us as well as the person who did them. I know this will take real courage, but it is such an important piece of recovery process. Our trust in God to help us here is all that gets us through.

If the person is not accessible, we can write a letter and share it with our support person. We can forgive as Christ did by releasing those who hurt us because they did not know what they were doing.

Expressing Significant Emotional Statements. I've heard many clients make statements like, "I never told him how much I loved him," "I really cared for her even though she hurt me," "I know he did the best he could, but I did not tell him." I encourage you to write down all of the things you wished you could have said. Get them on paper in front of you and decide how you want to express them. If the person is available, let them know. If not, share it with someone else. There have been many creative ways people have dealt with loss in this way.

☐ A daughter whose parents committed suicide composed a beautiful musical tape entitled "Learning to Let Go."

☐ A father who had a daughter die in his arms wrote poetry expressing the helplessness and tenderness he felt.

☐ A woman wrote a ten-page letter incorporating all of her forgiveness, amends and significant statements, then she burned each page and prayed as the smoke went heavenward, turning over all of her words to God to handle.

☐ A young man buried all of his drug paraphernalia and with the burial died to his old way of life.

☐ A woman revisited the gravesite of her husband, then talked and cried until she felt finished.

☐ A man drove three hundred miles to his father's restaurant where he was repeatedly abused and sat outside until he had the strength to go in and order a meal.

☐ A woman called a family meeting and read the letters she had written to each member.

☐ A father called his whole family together and sang a song about his failures and the love he has for his family.

It is important for each person to find out what is needed to complete the healing process and then have the courage to follow through.

A Final Note

Grief work takes time and no one can determine just how long the process will take. Many well-meaning friends can impair the process by encouraging us to hurry up or by asking just how long it will take. The rule of thumb is simply that we each take as long as we need. We are so afraid of falling into self-pity or being stuck in the pain that we try to rush ahead, "acting" like we are over the loss when we still hurt.

Grief is a natural healing process for the wounds of our heart. As we face the wound we begin that process. But be advised: many of our friends have not faced their losses. Seeing us in pain reminds them of the unresolved pain that lies buried. That is why it is important to find understanding support for our grief process.

Grief work is painful, but the release that can follow from the work is worth it all. Adult children from dysfunctional homes have a lot of sadness and loss to grow through in order to reclaim their future. Each of us that have gone through the losses find a broader vision of life and changed values. I pray that each of you continue your healing journey.

Suggested Readings

Melba Colgrove et al. 1983. *How to Survive the Loss of a Love.* New York: Bantam.

John W. James and Frank Cherry. 1989. *The Grief Recovery Handbook.* New York: Harper & Row.

Dennis Linn and Matthew Linn. 1978. *Healing Life's Hurts.* Mahwah, N.J.: Paulist Press.

Jane Middleton-Moz and Lorie Dwinell. 1986. *After the Tears.* Deerfield Beach, Fla.: Health Communications.

Carol Standacher. 1987. *Beyond Grief.* Oakland, Calif.: New Harbinger.

Philip Yancy. 1977. *Where Is God When It Hurts?* Grand Rapids, Mich.: Zondervan.

8

BUILDING AWARENESS OF OUR THOUGHTS

◆ ◆ ◆

I've read over and over from the recovery books that I make myself feel the way I feel and I control my feelings. So I should be able to stop what I feel and just feel better. But I can't. I don't know what to do. And then I get so angry with myself for not being able to control myself. I wonder if I'm damaged in my head or something. Others make it sound so simple, but it doesn't work for me. *George*

*E*very church service I attend the pastors tell me what I should be thinking and why I don't have good feelings about being a Christian. Many times they tell me to stop looking at what I feel and just believe I'm a new creation and all the old things will pass away. I act better around them, but they don't really know the real me. I don't feel any different on the inside. I just pretend more on the outside. I feel split down the middle and confused about how this Christianity stuff is any different from the messages I got in my family. Act right, don't talk, don't feel, be happy, don't be selfish and don't have problems. Sounds just like my family.　*Steve*

One can sense the frustration George and Steve both feel. They are sincerely attempting to recover but have been given an oversimplified message about perception changes.

Psychology has undergone a cognitive revolution in the last few years based on the works of Albert Ellis, Aaron Beck and others. The field of recovery has benefitted from understanding how important our thoughts are in how we feel and what we do. Religious teachers and authors have long established the role that beliefs and values contribute to our daily lives.

There seems to be, however, a greater emphasis placed on changing what we think so we can feel better. This ignores basic recovery principles of acceptance, comfort, expression of feelings and grief work. To do so can be devastating to our recovery. If we are in pain, we want a fix. Anyone who teaches that recovery is as easy as changing your mind fails to understand the trauma adult children from dysfunctional homes have encountered.

Without a focus in the three areas of thoughts, feelings and behavior we miss the work of our true spiritual journey. To focus only on one part, in exclusion of the others, limits our recovery. We have completed working through the AAA sequence for emotions in chapters four through seven. In this and the following chapters we are going to do the same with thoughts.

Epictetus said, "The problem lies not with the world but with our perception of the world." I would add that the problem is the fallen world we live in *and* our perceptions of it. In Romans 12:2 Paul wrote, "Do not conform any longer to the pattern of this world, but be transformed by the renewing of your mind." This means that our thoughts and perceptions can be changed. God can do this because, as Paul said in 2 Corinthians 10:5, we have weapons of divine power that can "take captive every thought to make it obedient to Christ."

All of the rules and messages we were given in childhood are contained in our thought life. These form our values and beliefs. Every event of life is processed by the way we think. Out of our thoughts flow feelings and decisions. If there is to be healing for ACAs, then perceptions and beliefs will need to be altered. The renewing of the mind is the adjustment of a person's beliefs to conform with the truth of God.

Automatic Thought Processes

Thoughts are learned. All of us have thousands of experiences and messages about ourselves, others and the world stored in our mind. All of these are learned. Sometimes they come as direct statements like, "We don't talk to others about what goes on in our family." This means, "Don't talk." Other times they are indirect messages such as a father's criticism of his son for not "standing up for himself." This means, "Real men fight and don't act scared." Sometimes it is a conclusion the child draws based upon what is felt. For example, a parent was angry at the child for making a mistake and yelled at the child, calling him or her stupid. This means, "I feel stupid. I must be stupid."

Sometimes the messages are recorded by watching the people around us and drawing conclusions. For example, a mother would have angry outbursts but was very inconsistent with which situations caused her anger. This means, "Always watch out, you can't trust people close to you." Or, "I am to blame for mother's feelings. I should do better."

Our mind contains countless messages. Many are very appropriate and help us to live and interact. However, there are messages that do not help us to grow, mature and lead lives that are productive. How we view life is learned at a very early age. Alfred Adler believed that we learn a style of life within the first years of childhood and live out the rest of life fulfilling the self-perceptions.

Many of our thoughts become automatic. For instance, getting dressed in the morning most of us give little thought to simple tasks such as tying our shoes, buttoning our clothes or tucking in a shirt or blouse. As a matter of fact, we are able to talk, watch a television show or perform some other task while we dress. We have learned how to dress and have repeated the task so often it has become automatic. Yet, below our awareness level the mind is organizing the body to perform the appropriate steps needed in order to get dressed. We only become aware of what we are doing when something is not fitting correctly. Like slipping into our shoes and finding the right shoe is going on the left foot. It does not fit and we become aware and then alter the dressing process.

In the same way, we have automatic thoughts we have learned about ourselves, others and the world. These thoughts have been taught to us and have been repeated in our mind enough to become automatic. We are unaware that we are even thinking about anything. We may just see what we do and experience a feeling, but not know that we have automatic thoughts. These automatic thoughts are made up of all our messages and rules. They become our belief system, that which is "true" to us.

We all have belief systems. They help us to organize the world around us. They help us to categorize all the stimuli the environment brings to us. They give meaning to the events that happen to us.

Thoughts tend to go together. For instance, suppose Ruth just received notice that she was turned down for a job she hoped to get. She would likely have several thoughts such as, "What's wrong with me?" "I'll never get a good job." "I needed this job." "How will I face my family?" "I can't stand rejection." Rarely does a person only make one statement in response to any event. Over time our thoughts form what I call clusters which seem to show up together. Identifying our clusters or the patterns that we learned is an essential piece of our recovery work.

The mind acts as a recorder and stores away all the previous experiences that are significant. Then, in response to an event the mind evaluates the situation using the previously recorded material. In this way the person can "make sense out of the event."

Since the beliefs are automatic and true to us, they are rarely challenged. They are rarely tested by reality because most of the time we are unaware of what we really believe or why we believe what we believe. When we look at our prejudice and bias, we end up with a conclusion that is loosely supported by rationalization. But the honest statement is, "That's just the way I believe."

On the road to healing, many of us find that our beliefs about life are really our parents' messages and rules which they inherited from their parents. Recovery offers an opportunity to discover what we believe and determine what is helpful and what hinders us. This gives us a chance to build a more effective belief system to live our lives by.

Because our belief patterns are learned at such an early age, breaking them is sometimes a slow process. It is like reading about a better way of thinking but finding that just reading about it does not seem to be enough to change our thoughts. We need to remind ourselves that the beliefs are part of our core outlook about life and therefore deeply attached to us. Changing them does require a consistent and strong approach. Sometimes, however, our perceptions can change quickly. Let me give two examples.

Jack's Encounter

Jack, who is now in his late fifties, was raised in the Deep South and was prejudiced against many races but in particular against the Black race. He believed Blacks could not be trusted, "weren't any good for anything," and were never as good as "White folks."

On a recent fishing trip to the Cascade Mountains his car broke down. While walking out of a very remote area, Jack fell and broke his leg. While he agonized in pain and spent a lot of time in prayer asking God for help, the hours passed slowly. Jack had almost given up hope when he heard someone walking by the stream down below him. He cried out for help and the man yelled back to just hold on until he could get there. Jack's hopes were raised because help was on its way. He thanked God for answering his prayers. But Jack was not prepared for what would happen.

The man came around the trail and immediately began to help Jack. Jack's response turned from hope to disgust because the man was Black. The intense feelings of disdain filled him rapidly. Here was Jack in anguish and pain, unable to help himself, and a Black man was helping him. He discovered just how deeply rooted his bias was. Later he confessed that he thought, "Don't touch me. You're Black. I'll wait for someone else." The man helped him form a splint, carried him up to the road, and took him to a hospital. He returned to Jack's car with a buddy, fixed it and drove it to the hospital.

Jack and this man are friends today and share many common interests, especially fishing in the Cascades. Jack has often told his friends, and anyone else who'll listen, that the real healing that he experienced was not his broken bone. But, rather, his blinded attitude and crippled heart. He believed that when he cried out because of his pain, God answered, and brought healing to the anguish he felt.

Our automatic thought processes can be described as our inner voice or self-talk. We can learn to identify and capture our inner dialog by asking ourselves, "What am I saying to myself?" This is the first step of awareness in the AAA format. What follows is an exercise that can help us with this. I'll end the chapter with a list of rules, messages and perceptions common to many ACAs. Chapters nine and ten will contain specific strategies to aid in altering our self-talk.

Reality Snapshot

Developing awareness is difficult, but no more difficult than living in ignorance of what is really going on in us and around us. If we are going to break free from conditioned and habitual patterns, we need to develop a tool for discovery. Yet this tool must allow us the flexibility to move beyond discovery into real recovery. Look at the visual representation in figure 2 of what I call a Reality Snapshot.

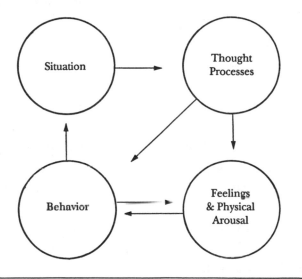

Figure 2. *A Reality Snapshot*

Briefly let's look at this snapshot. First, something happens (a situation). This is processed automatically (thought processes). Then, there is an emotional response (feelings and physical arousal) which results in action (behavior).

This may sound technical, so let's return to the snapshot and add the questions we need to ask in order to build our awareness (figure 3).

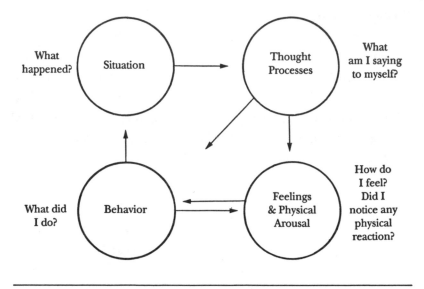

Figure 3. *A Reality Snapshot with Questions*

Think of a situation where you felt uncomfortable. Now ask yourself the following questions:

  What happened?

  How did I feel?

  Did I notice any physical reaction?

  What did I do?

  What am I saying to myself about the situation?

If you completed this exercise, you have taken a Reality Snapshot.

While traveling on the freeway after work, a car cut in front of me and almost hit me. I reacted with anger and tried to catch the crazy maniac. I pulled off the freeway and drove into a parking lot to take a Reality Snapshot to record my self-talk. I wrote the following:

  What happened? A driver cut in front of me on the freeway.

  How did I feel? Angry, scared, shocked.

  Did I notice any physical reaction? Yes, my body was wired. My heart was beating fast. I was breathing with short breaths.

What did I do? I drove fast. I yelled at him. I tried hard to catch him and give him a piece of my mind.

What am I saying to myself? He shouldn't drive that way. What's wrong with people today? He is an idiot and I should let him know just how lousy he is at driving. I can't stand people that drive that way. What did I do to deserve this after a hard day at work? He could have caused an accident.

After taking my snapshot, I took a few minutes to breathe slower and prayed for help in calming myself down. Needless to say, I was not a happy camper. But after comforting myself I did feel better and the intensity passed. I encourage you to use this exercise often in the AAA recovery format to build awareness. I find it very useful in exposing my self-talk.

This exercise can be used for current or past situations. While the situation I used as an illustration was not particularly intense for me, many that I wrote about were more difficult. Once we get a clear understanding of our self-talk, we can begin the process of altering our inner self-dialog. Sometimes, when we see our self-talk written down for the first time, we have trouble accepting that the words really reflect our beliefs. But they do. We act and feel consistently with the internal self-talk that we believe the most.

Ineffective Rules and Messages

To sharpen your awareness of your thought patterns, consider some negative rules and messages typical ACAs heard from their families.

Rules	*Messages*
Don't feel.	You are bad, stupid, selfish.
Don't talk.	Your feelings don't count.
Don't trust.	Grow up.
Don't ask questions.	What's wrong with you?
Don't be yourself.	You aren't like _____ .

Don't betray the family.	You don't hurt.
Don't lose control.	You'll never amount to anything.
Don't question those in authority.	You don't know anything.
Don't talk about alcohol.	Shame on you.
Keep the family secrets.	You are embarrassing us.

Rules and messages like these are stored in our memory. They contribute to the beliefs we hold about ourselves, others and the world. They contribute to our low self-esteem and keep us stuck in our pain.

As you take your Reality Snapshot, be alert to these negative messages and rules reflected in your self-talk. It is not your fault that you have them. It is your responsibility to expose them and decide how you will alter them.

In closing, I remind you to practice using acceptance and comfort as you look honestly at your self-talk. You are not bad or unworthy because you have such thoughts. They are a result of your dysfunctional family of origin. No one is to be blamed or be shamed.

As you reveal them, you move to a position to take action and change what you believe. For the first time in your life, you will decide how and what you will believe.

9
RENEWING OUR MINDS: CHALLENGING OUR SELF-TALK

♦ ♦ ♦

I am taking more time for myself now. When feelings come up inside me I don't avoid them like I used to do. I don't like to have feelings, but I keep giving myself permission to feel. It seems like sometimes the feelings go away after I talk with myself. I try to let myself know that the feelings are normal and that they will pass. That they are within me for good reasons and are a signal to me so I can pay attention to myself and what is happening to me. This has really helped me to not feel so bad. Also, I notice the feelings aren't as intense after I talk nice with myself.

My problem is that I really don't want to keep having the fears I have, but I don't know how to get rid of them. Am I going to spend my life in fear? I understand fear is OK, but it sure seems like I get afraid over a lot of little things. Like the other day when I couldn't see my boy on the playground. I immediately was terrified. I started breathing fast and looking everywhere for him. I started to panic. I began to calm myself down, breathe slower and accept my feelings. Then I saw him walk out of the rest room. I asked him where he had been. He replied, "Mommy, I had to go potty." I was thankful, but later thought to myself, "Will I ever get to the point where I won't always be terrified over such things?" Isn't there something I could do that will help me more than what I'm doing now? *Carla*

Carla is using some good recovery tools to help her deal with the fears and panic that she has lived with for years. As a child she was often abandoned by her family, left alone at night and abused physically by her father when he would come home drunk. Carla's world was a life of terror and chaos. She lived with her fears as constant companions. She couldn't trust in the people around her to create safety. She learned to never depend upon them but was overwhelmed with her fears. "After all," she concluded, "how could I as a six-year-old know what I really should be doing to take better care of myself? I was so busy trying to keep from being afraid that I didn't have any time to think about anything else."

Carla is interested in making deeper changes. She is walking along her journey and building on the earlier recovery strategies. She has spent time discovering her feelings and her family of origin. She writes in a diary, attends a support group, participates in a church fellowship and has developed an important relationship with a friend. She spends time accepting her feelings and works on the losses she feels from her childhood. All of the work she has done is vital and will need to be a continued part of her recovery plan.

Now Carla is ready to move on and add more techniques such as the ones found in this chapter and the next. In this chapter, I will present eight major styles of thinking that create distress. And I will develop confrontation strategies one can use to alter ineffective self-talk.

I would caution you to realize that changing deeply held ideas and perspectives will require more than reading about them or just understanding the thoughts. It will take practice to be able to break the old patterns and substitute new, more healthy patterns.

Challenging What We Think

In chapter eight I mentioned that most of our beliefs are rarely challenged. In this section we will look at some specific thought patterns and build strategies that will help us to challenge the parts of our inner dialog that create distress. For some of you examining your thought patterns in this way will seem awkward and unnatural.

At the same time, this process is very natural. We do it often without calling it a therapeutic technique. Let me give an example. While driving to a lunch appointment you look down at your watch and calculate you will probably be ten minutes late. In response to this insight, you begin to speed and feel tense. You think to yourself, "I can't be later. I should always be on time. They will think I'm not very organized." Then you think, "Wait a minute. I am not going to jeopardize my good driving record by risking a ticket for speeding. I guess I won't be on time for this appointment. I don't like that, but I can live with it. If they are real upset, I will handle that as well. I will apologize for any inconvenience and let it go. In the future I will try to plan for more time in between appointments." Then you resume a normal speed and feel calmer.

What took place was a confrontation within yourself between two thought patterns. One created tension and led to high-risk behavior. The other faced reality and led to less tension and more appropriate behavior. This normal process that goes unnoticed is what the cognitive therapists have fine-tuned to assist us in the recovery process. Although I don't want to sound simplistic with the techniques, many are based upon emotional common sense.

All of our beliefs are formed by parental, cultural and peer expectations and by our needs to feel loved, to belong and to feel safe. Our beliefs represent our values. Some help us to live in a constructive manner. Others are inflexible and life-restricting. We will learn to challenge these and reduce the power they hold over us. Unhealthy self-talk continues the dysfunction from our family of origin. The negative rules and messages presented in chapter eight can be seen throughout the following patterns. Each of the patterns listed reflects self-talk that creates distress for us and hinders our path to healing.

1. Absolute Thinking

Thinking in absolutes is a form of perfectionism. Using words like *should* or *ought, must* or *have-to* are often a reflection of rigid rules for living. Absolutes that don't exist create anger and shame. Here are some common examples of ineffective absolutes:

- ☐ You must be perfect or you are bad.
- ☐ Others ought to be perfect.
- ☐ You shouldn't talk about the family secrets.
- ☐ You shouldn't cry, ask questions, think of yourself.

Take a minute and list some of your own absolute thoughts.

- ☐ You should _____ .
- ☐ Life must _____ .

Reasonable and appropriate expectations form a healthy value system. We need a moral code to direct our path. I am primarily labeling shoulds as dysfunctional when they are shaming, blaming and perfectionistic. These shoulds beg the question of reality and demand an ideal world that just doesn't exist.

Let's return to Carla. When she felt fearful she caught herself saying, "I shouldn't be afraid. I'm a grown adult." Then she felt bad because she was fearful. The cause of her feeling bad was the belief that she shouldn't feel afraid. She was repeating to herself exactly what her parents had told her for years.

To challenge this belief she gained a basic understanding that feelings are a part of being human and that in order to heal she needed to give herself permission to feel. She learned that demanding she shouldn't feel, when in fact she does, is denying reality. Thus her expectations kept her from dealing with her fears, and created more intense feelings of badness. Her homework looked like the following:

What happened: I was afraid.

How did I feel: angry and bad.

What did I do: nothing.

What am I saying to myself: I shouldn't be afraid. I'm a grown adult. There must be something wrong with me.

Adapting and challenging:

1. There is no law that I can't feel.

2. Feelings are part of being human. I'm not bad. I'm just human.

3. Stop demanding that something not exist that does exist.

4. I don't like to be afraid, but I can face it. If only for a few minutes.

5. My fears are a signal to me but I don't know what they mean yet.

6. Breathe slower and this too will pass.

Carla's challenges helped her calm down. She still felt fear, but the badness and blame subsided.

Much as we all believe that there is no such thing as a perfect person, many ACAs demand perfection in themselves and expect others to be perfect as well.

To comfort yourself in facing your desire for perfection you can use the following challenges:

1. Does believing this help me or hinder me?

2. Does this make me feel good or bad?

3. Is there any evidence for the falseness of this idea?

4. Is this a true reality-based statement?

5. Is there a law that says this belief exists?

One final note about absolutes. Many of our expectations are values we want to live by. They are healthy and reflect the way we want to treat ourselves and others. When we violate them, we feel guilty, and the only way to relieve the feeling is through forgiveness, atonement and letting go.

In the 12-step literature, step five encourages us to admit to God, ourselves and another human being the exact nature of our wrongs. This is similar to confessing our sins to one another (James 5:16). Step eight encourages us to make a list of all the people we have harmed and become willing to make amends to them all. Mark 11:25 says that if we hold anything against anyone we are to forgive that person. I believe this applies to ourselves as well. We need to practice forgiving ourselves daily.

Step ten encourages us to take personal inventory and where we are wrong promptly admit it. Matthew 5:25 talks about settling matters quickly. More than once I have seen relapse occur in my life and in the lives of others because we simply failed to follow a path of forgiveness to release ourselves from the wrongs we commit.

2. All-or-Nothing Thinking

In black-and-white thinking, or dichotomous thinking, there is no middle ground. There is no room for mistakes.

☐ I am either great or terrible.

☐ If I am not perfect, then I'm a complete failure.

☐ Friends must always be for me or they are against me.

☐ My spouse cares for me or hates me.

A helpful technique in challenging this way of thinking is to use percentages.

☐ The meal was 50% good instead of the dinner was complete garbage.

☐ The party wasn't a total flop. Over half of the guests had a good time, 20% were unhappy and 20% I'm not real sure about.

☐ My husband isn't a totally uncaring person. Rather he is a person that cares for me 60% of the time, doesn't act caring 20% of the time, and 20% of the time does things that have little to do with caring.

☐ Rather than believing I am totally incompetent on the job after making a mistake, I say I am highly competent 50% of the time, average 40% of the time and incompetent 10% of the time.

All-or-nothing thinking is a form of absolute thinking. Absolute thinkers believe there are only two options to whatever they are facing. The options are perfection or total failure. By building upon the questions listed in the section on absolute thinking and adding the concept of percentages, we can be more realistic about what has happened. Our energy is spent more wisely on the situation we face, rather than the discouragement and self-blame that normally occur when we talk to ourselves with black-and-white statements.

3. Being Right

In families where there were a lot of rigid rules and criticism that promoted shame, children learned that being right was vital to not feeling bad. As adults, many are still trying to defend their fragile sense of self-worth by continuing to prove the rightness of their ideas and behavior. Any criticism by others is a criticism of their self-worth. To admit to failure is admitting that they are a failure. The key statement at the heart of the belief is, "If I am wrong, then I must be bad."

Couples that both believe this statement will find themselves lost in a constant battle of defending nearly everything they think, feel and do. They will be in turmoil searching for who was right. One speaker I heard called this the "truth-seeking dance." The idea that one must be right carries the sting someone must be wrong. It is a dance of winning and losing with both eventually losing the sense of self-esteem, recognition and acceptance they both need.

Key challenges that build on the earlier questions we mentioned about absolutes are:

☐ Is it possible to be right all of the time?

☐ Making mistakes is part of being human.

☐ I don't like to goof, but I have to accept that I've made errors and survived.

☐ I need to learn to build my self-esteem in other ways without always being right.

☐ There is no one that hasn't made mistakes. All of us have experienced being wrong.

4. Indecision

Living in a home with chaos, where the rules were constantly changing, can produce a sense of deep insecurity and doubt. You can never count on yourself as a thinker and trust in your decision-making ability. One day it was OK to stay at the friend's home and play. The next day father was angry and punished everyone for going to the friend's home. The indecision from childhood becomes a way of processing life. Children learned in a state of fear to avoid a decision out of fear. Others around would insist on the "correct" decision or would be quick to blame the child for the "wrong" decision. Either way children learn to distrust the natural ability to think and test out reality.

Another issue with indecision is the fear of making a wrong choice. And with the wrong choice comes punishment for being bad. So at the heart of indecision is the conclusion that "if I choose wrongly, I will be punished and feel shame."

The inability to make mistakes, together with the changing rules, creates a sense of distrust, doubt, fear and shame. Children raised in this atmosphere often become very anxious as adults.

The internal self-talk is characterized by a series of what-ifs. The endless dialog with indecisive thinking feels much like you are the ball in a tennis match. Back and forth . . . this option, then the other . . . this way, then that way, the dialog continues.

The key areas to build confronting strategies are as follows:

☐ Realize that when we do not make a decision between options, a decision is still being made. In other words, not to decide is to decide.

☐ Attack the idea that you must make the perfect choice or you are bad.

☐ Realizing that indecision takes the focus off tough decisions and contributes to avoiding life's difficult situations. Some of us really do believe it is better to avoid than to face life's difficult situations.

☐ Learn to accept the fears we have and still move forward to a decision point. Often we are trying to avoid our fear and yet do not understand that fear is fueled by our indecision.

☐ Use the question: "What is the worst that could happen to me if I made a wrong choice?" Often the very thing we fear is the fear itself.

5. Obsessive Thinking about the Past

After breaking through denial, many adult children constantly ruminate over the past. Often this process is resolved by sharing the early memories and past experiences and then moving through the AAA stages of healing.

When we look at obsessive thinking patterns, however, we are viewing a style of thinking rather than just the early awareness phenomena. It may reflect an unresolved issue such as, "I cannot stop thinking about the divorce." Or, "I keep returning in my mind to what Daddy did to me, and I just feel awful." Sometimes it reflects situations that need a decision. Such as, "I keep going around and around with whether or not I should quit my job." Or, "I know I should talk to my Dad, but I just can't."

Sometimes it reflects messages given to us by our parents that we cannot break. Such as, "I'm just no good." Or others like, "I'm stupid, shouldn't feel, can't grow up or will never be good enough." Nearly any pattern of thinking can become an obsessive pattern.

In order to break the patterns let me give three recommendations. First, for unresolved issues you will need to take the time to understand the deeper underlying feelings and to realize that healing the wounds will resolve a great deal of the obsessive thoughts. Second, for indecisive issues, you can use some of the techniques listed previously for indecision. Third, for obsessive messages, you will need to learn a technique called thought-stopping which I'll discuss further in the next chapter.

6. Hypervigilance

Something awful could happen.

They might laugh at me.

If someone saw me make a mistake, I couldn't stand it.

I have to always watch out and not be caught off guard.

I have to make sure everyone around me is happy.

I can tell by their faces, they don't like my new hairdo.

Hypervigilance is very common for adult children. Learning to "read" the environment, the feelings of others and potential dangerous situations, was vital to surviving in the home. If one could respond with the right survival behavior, then worse circumstances could be avoided.

For instance, in an alcoholic home, children learned when to ask the parents for things they wanted. There was a right time to ask and a bad time to ask. Learning the difference was important to not only get more of what was wanted but also to avoid the anger and chaos. The problem for children was that they did not realize that the rules would change more often than they could keep up with them. What became most predictable was unpredictability. In attempting to avoid distressing situations, they did not understand that there was no escape from the distress.

So adult children become like sentries on guard duty in a war zone. Always watching, ever vigilant, constantly on guard for a breakout of the crazies in the family. Adult children repeat over and over, "If there is something that might happen that is worrisome or dangerous, then I must worry about it." And, "If it happened, it would be awful."

We are not going to deal in a full manner with all the issues that potentially exist. However, let's look at some challenges clients have found helpful.

☐ We need to learn to confront the whole notion of just how tragic the current situation really is. By listening to ourselves we hear a lot of self-talk that uses the key words *terrible, awful, devastating* and *totally bad.* While it is true our experiences may have been tragic, many situations we currently face are not tragic.

☐ Replace the use of the words I mentioned with a less tragic language, such as *difficult, very hard, a real hassle, inconvenient* or *a tough situation.* While the use of this type of self-talk will not feel right, you need to realize that the other self-talk is probably creating many of the awful feelings you already experience.

☐ Recognize the distinction between what has happened in your childhood, which may be tragic, and what you are facing today, which may not be tragic at all.

☐ Learn to depend upon the fact that you did survive very difficult situations and are a survivor. You will face and live through today as well. Removing the negative self-talk will reduce the intensity you feel now, but not the effects of the early childhood trauma. This helps us to use the strength within us to move forward and face today, and learn to resolve the past.

☐ When my signal of fear goes off inside me, I learn to respond to the alarm and take a look at what is happening within me and around me. The key is trying to remove the distress of creating a more tragic situation by my self-talk.

☐ Where there are situations I think about that are truly tragic, such as anticipating someone's death, I try to emphasize the skills for survival I possess. Also, I try to build my sense of acceptance about death.

☐ Sometimes breaking the pattern needs professional help because we may feel really out of control to alter the process. If you notice after some effort that the pattern is too strong, get professional help.

7. Overgeneralization

When one particular of a situation leads us to make a broad, unwarranted conclusion, we have overgeneralized. The key words in such conclusions are *always, everybody, nobody, never.* For example:

☐ Nobody will ever go out with me [after being turned down once].

☐ I never get anything right.

☐ Everybody thinks I'm a loser.

☐ If people really know me, they wouldn't love me.

☐ Recovery is too hard. I'll never understand.

☐ I'll never change.

☐ I'll never get a better job.

☐ All people who treat me unfairly are bad and should be punished.

There are times when the use of these words is correct. Such as, "My father passed away, and I will never be able to fish with him again." In situations like this there is no need to confront the key word because it is true. But when our overgeneralizations cause us to lose hope and become discouraged, when they trap us in a vicious circle of putting ourselves down, or when they lead to avoiding our real problems, then it is time to challenge them.

Since the variety of statements could be endless, I'll give a representative sample of generalizations with a useful confronting technique for each one.

1. "I never get anything right." In my whole life I've *never* gotten anything right? There isn't any *one* time I was correct in my behavior? Rather, "I didn't get it right this time and that doesn't feel good. But I can learn from this mistake."

2. "Everybody thinks I'm a loser." Everybody? Everybody you have ever met called you a loser? There isn't one that holds a different opinion? Also, another strategy would be: What do I think about me? If I see myself as a total failure (loser), then it really doesn't matter what others think. I'm so busy beating up on me, others wouldn't have a chance.

3. "Nobody will ever go out with me." Two key words need to be confronted. *Nobody* and *ever.* Nobody? Have you asked everyone out? Or isn't the truth, this particular person I just asked said no. And this is hard to deal with right now. But you say this is the third rejection. Three still doesn't mean nobody will go out with me. Ever? The rest of my entire life?

4. "I will always be a failure." Always? I know for certain how the rest of my life is going to go? I can predict the future so well as to confirm that I will always fail in everything I tackle? Rather, today I failed at something and I don't feel great about it. But I can go on from here and use what I learn from this failure.

It is clear that confronting these words takes some work and creativity. But with practice we can diminish the use of overgeneralizations.

Overgeneralizations are often tied together with other evaluations. For instance, "I'll never understand this recovery process" and "That is awful." Or, "Nobody will ever go out with me" and "I'm such a terrible person." Both may need to be confronted because of the distressing feelings that are generated from such beliefs.

8. Personalization

The last type of negative self-talk, personalization, compares ourselves to others or associates with what are actually unrelated comments about ourselves.

☐ Everyone is better than I.

☐ She is smarter than I.

☐ I'm really dumb compared to her.

☐ Other clients must be better at this than I.

☐ When my wife talks about not having enough money for food, I'm sure she thinks I don't provide well enough.

☐ When my husband comments about another woman's clothes, I'm sure he thinks I'm ugly.

The key in recognizing personalizing statements is watching for comparisons that devalue our self-esteem. The themes are: others are better than me; others think I'm not good enough; or I'll never be good enough.

Once we begin to recognize the statements we make to ourselves, we have to stop them in order to stop the shaming. Thought stopping is an important technique. So is building a strong affirmation script to help stabilize the wounded feelings day by day. I'll present both techniques in the following chapter.

10
RENEWING OUR MINDS: MORE STRATEGIES

♦ ♦ ♦

*F*inally, brothers, whatever is true, whatever is noble, whatever is right, whatever is pure, whatever is lovely, whatever is admirable—if anything is excellent or praiseworthy—think about such things.
Philippians 4:8

---

*I*t feels uncomfortable for me to say nice things about myself. Dad always told me that it was wrong to brag. Besides I heard my Sunday-school teacher tell us the other day we shouldn't talk about ourselves. I'll try to do the homework, but it doesn't feel good. I guess this sounds pretty silly. I came for counseling because I felt lousy about myself. Now I feel lousy trying to learn how to feel better about myself. **Ken, a twenty-two-year-old ACA**

ACAs, and those raised in dysfunctional families, have a view of themselves, others and the world that is in need of healing. If you find it difficult to use the tools recommended in this book, please take heart. All of us in recovery have struggled to adapt our rules, alter our messages and heal our memories. It helps to reach out to others in recovery and talk with a pastor or therapist.

Meditation and Visualization

What comes to your mind when the word *visualization* is mentioned? There is considerable debate, pro and con, about it. Visualization forms the basis for our thought processes. It can be used to escape reality, such as a daydream. Or it can be used to create significant inner healing. It can be used to destroy the health of the inner person and produce a life of disregard for others. Or it can be used to heal our memories and free us from condemnation. We need to ask the purpose behind the use of visualization to determine the value. Any approach can be used or misused. Investigate with me the healthy use of this technique.

Visualization is a thought process. It is the forming of mental pictures or images in our minds. Mental pictures can recreate a situation and play it in our minds like a movie. Visualizing is a reconstruction of a significant event we have stored in our memories.

I have heard often that all of our thoughts become our reality. People do not experience the world as it is but rather how it is perceived within their minds. Our best feelings today come from memories where we felt accepted and loved. Developing the skill of visualization is essential to complete healing because all of us have memories that affect us today.

Sports, medicine and religion have used visualization techniques for years. More evidence is being generated substantiating its healthy use in the treatment of stress, chronic pain, headaches, ulcers and other symptoms.

Pause for a moment and think about an award or prize you once received or a birthday party you were given. Stop and think about the event. Try to remember everything you can about it. Who was there? What did you get? Where did this happen? Did they sing for you? Was there cheering? Were there lots of smiles? Try to fully remember the event.

Now stop and get in touch with how you feel. Most of us will experience pleasant emotions. For a moment we return in our feelings to the earlier situation.

For many ACAs, the birthday party was an unpleasant experience. The feelings are of sadness, loss and hurt. There was no gift. Nobody remembered my birthday. No matter what you recalled, you have feelings about the situation. That is the power of visualizing. When we recall an event, how we felt then is experienced today.

The question is not whether or not we should visualize, but rather *what* do we picture in our mind. Learning to picture healthy and appropriate scenes to replace the hurtful scenes is the key. Whether or not you believe in the technique will not stop the effectiveness once you try it.

A Scriptural Perspective

The Bible shows that the wrong use of our minds and imagination is evil and dark. "The Lord saw that the wickedness of man was great in the earth, and that every imagination of the thoughts of his heart was only evil continually" (Genesis 6:5, Amplified). Ephesians 4:17-18 says, "So I tell you this, and insist on it in the Lord, that you must no longer live as the Gentiles do, in the futility of their thinking. They are darkened in their understanding and separated from the life of God because of the ignorance that is in them due to the hardening of their hearts."

God knows our thoughts. But we can break through our denial by telling him what we think. I think God knew we would struggle with our thoughts. That is why there are so many references to our thought life in Scripture.

The Bible is also full of rich imagery we can use in a positive and healing manner. There are numerous stories, parables and illustrations recorded for our benefit. Read the following portions I've selected and try to image the mental pictures conveyed.

"How great is your goodness, . . . on those who take refuge in you. . . . in your dwelling you keep them safe from accusing tongues" (Psalm 31:19-22).

"He lifted me out of the slimy pit, out of the mud and mire, he set my feet on a rock and gave me a firm place to stand" (Psalm 40:2-3).

"The LORD is with me; I will not be afraid. What can man do to me?" (Psalm 118:6).

"Fear of man will prove to be a snare, but whoever trusts in the LORD is kept safe" (Proverbs 29:25).

"He will cover you with his feathers, and under his wings you will find refuge; his faithfulness will be your shield and rampart. You will not fear the terror of night, nor the arrow that flies by day, nor the pestilence that stalks in the darkness, nor the plague that destroys at midday" (Psalm 91:4-5).

"The LORD is my shepherd, I shall not be in want. He makes me lie down in green pastures, he leads me beside quiet waters, he restores my soul. He guides me in paths of righteousness for his name's sake. Even though I walk through the valley of the shadow of death, I will fear no evil, for you are with me; your rod and your staff, they comfort me" (Psalm 23:1-4).

Many times in the Old Testament God encourages his people to remember the experiences they had, to meditate and dwell on the great events of the exodus from Egypt, the parting of the Red Sea and the fulfillment of giving them the Promised Land. These events are virtually impossible to remember without a visual picture coming to mind. God knew that dwelling on such pictures in a healthy, constructive manner can build into us an appreciation of who God is and what he has done for us. Visualizing can heal our memories, eliminate self-hate, provide comfort and draw us closer to God.

The following exercises help us visualize in positive ways. First is one way to help us relax and be calm. The next will be to help us build a skill, change a behavior or some negative self-talk. The last one shows one way we can heal our memories.

Relaxing and Calming Visualization

Step 1. Think about a time when you felt relaxed, safe or comforted. It can be as simple as a day fishing, being held by your grandmother or sitting in a hot tub. It does not matter. Just use one that is best for you in this exercise.

Step 2. Write out all that you can remember about this relaxing time. Here's what I remember about one of my favorite relaxing scenes, a hot tub. In thinking about it I want to remember all that I could about each of my senses. Smell—does the water smell like chlorine? Sight—color of the hot tub? Where is it located? Do I see the bubbles? Hearing—can I hear the water rushing around me? Any other noises? Taste—did I get some water in my mouth? How did it taste? Touch —do I feel the heat of the water and the pulsating air jets pushing against me? Now you have a better picture of the hot tub scene to use in your relaxation scene.

Step 3. Sit down in a comfortable chair or lie down. Plan for a few minutes to be alone and uninterrupted.

Step 4. First, breathe slowly and take deep breaths of air. Breathe in through your nose and out through your mouth. Take several breaths and each time you breathe out say the word *relax* or *calm.*

Step 5. Picture your comfortable scene. Try to capture all the various parts of the scene. Relive the time. Emphasize the warmth, relaxation, comfort and good feelings. Continue the deep breathing and focusing on everything positive about the scene. Do this as long as you want.

Step 6. As you bring the visualization to an end, repeat positive statements about the experience to yourself. Such as, "This was very good. I enjoyed this a lot. I like to calm down. It feels good to relax. It's nice to take time out for me. Next time this will be easier for me." Each of these statements will help anchor the exercise. By doing this you will be preparing yourself for the next time you use this exercise.

Step 7. Plan to do the exercise at least once a day for a week. The key is to keep practicing and building up the skill. The benefit of this exercise is your relaxation after each practice session.

You can use any healthy scene for yourself. Or you can build your own scene if you can't remember any. Take a warm bubble bath; go to a nice beach; go to a park, lake, stream, mountain or symphony. For some it will be useful to take some of the Scriptures I presented and build a comforting scene around the images they convey. Whatever you do, record the event for future use. Then go through the steps I've outlined. The primary goal of this type of visualization is to relax, comfort and calm our stress.

Skill-Building Visualization

The second type of visualization is skill building. In this technique you can work on any area of your life you choose. It might be practicing a new behavior, breaking an old one, increasing self-esteem or looking toward the future, seeing goals accomplished. Whatever you pick as the target, use the following steps as a structure to utilize visualization as a part of your recovery process.

Step 1. Pick the behavior or skill you desire to build.

Step 2. Identify a situation when the problem exists.

Step 3. Sit down in a comfortable chair.

Step 4. Relax by breathing slowly and using calming statements.

Step 5. Picture the scene where the problem occurs. Then replay the scene with you accomplishing what you need to do. Repeat the relaxing response and then repeat this step again.

Step 6. End the exercise with positive statements such as: "Next time this will be easier." "I'm getting better at building my skills." "Breaking my pattern is difficult, but with practice this will work."

Step 7. Plan the next time you will practice this exercise. Many have found it useful to record these sessions and keep track of the progress made as well as the specific targeted item.

Let me give an example. Bill had attended support group meetings for months and was well on his road to recovery. He was able to identify many patterns in need of changes and was spending time to develop and continue his growth process.

One of the patterns Bill wanted to change was his inability to say no to people. The specific situation involved some buddies of his who were still active in drinking too much. Even though Bill was clean and sober, they would ask him to join them at some of their boating parties. He knew going with them would risk his sobriety.

When he did not follow through with what he knew was best for him, he would feel angry at himself and feel worthless. When he could not say no he had thoughts like, "I should not hurt anyone's feelings. They will think I'm no good. They may never ask me to be with them again. I'll never have any more friends."

Bill had determined that two areas were in need of skill building. First, stronger challenges to his distortions. Second, standing up to his buddies when they asked him to go with them. To prepare for this exercise, he spent some time writing out his challenges to the ineffective patterns. He would use these during the visualization exercise.

Bill was now ready to practice. He sat down and slowly breathed to help calm down and focus his concentration. Then he pictured the situation. He could see his buddies coming down the street toward his house. They were in the truck pulling the boat. They were yelling and shouting, "Bill, let's go boating." Bill could feel some tension rise so he would pause and breathe slowly and calm himself down. Then he would proceed.

He saw himself walking to the door, standing tall, feeling confident. The whole time he was repeating to himself the challenge he had written out previously. "This is good for me. If they think I'm no good, they aren't my friends. Making good choices is difficult, but I can do it. This will be over soon and I'm going to feel great telling them no. Taking care of myself is more important than what those buddies think about me." Over and over Bill repeated his new perspective to himself.

He saw himself open the door and greet his buddies. "Come on, Bill, let's go boating," they said.

Bill took a deep breath and said, "No, I won't be going boating with you."

They laughed and replied, "Crap! Bill, you're going with us and that's the end of it."

"No!" Bill shouted, "I won't be going with you guys." And then he closed the door.

Over and over he repeated this. Only now he would add, "I did it. I finally told them no and I feel great. Taking care of me is important. If I need to call a friend in recovery I will. I need to share this victory."

Bill would end his scene by debriefing himself with statements such as, "This has been difficult, but with practice I'll get stronger. I am getting better at taking care of myself. Next time this will be easier."

I hope that you will practice the behaviors and internal messages you want to change using this or a similar technique. You will be amazed at the results. Remember, each time you practice is one more time you are storing in your memory banks the ability to act differently. The value of this technique is tremendous. You can practice countless times and get stronger in a desired behavior change or changes in internal self-talk. It can really prepare you for new behaviors.

In Bill's case, by the time he did confront his buddies, he had practiced at least twenty times. He was nervous but did follow through. I still remember his surprise. "I did it, I did it, I did it. I just can't believe it," he exclaimed. For Bill it was a victory. Now, he would use this victory as evidence that he can take better care of himself in other situations where he needs to assert himself.

Healing of Memories

Step 1. Recall a time when you were hurt.

Step 2. Write out all that you can remember about the event. What happened? What were your feelings? What did you do? What thoughts ran through your head? What conclusions did you draw from the event?

Step 3. Decide what you needed at the time. We cannot change the behavior of others. What happened to us is a fact. But we did need something we did not get. Usually protection, comfort, safety, positive statements, and meaningful touches were missing. Whatever it was, record it.

Step 4. Sit down in a comfortable chair or lie down. Plan for a few minutes to be alone.

Step 5. Begin the deep breathing and calming statements as in previous exercises.

Step 6. Picture the scene. Use the notes you've written to fully imagine the event.

Step 7. Bring into your scene your image of God or Christ. Make him as real as you can. Have him give to you what you needed. Perhaps it is a hug. Have him do it. Or maybe you needed to hear you are OK and not to blame for the actions of your parent. Have him tell you. Perhaps you needed to know this hurt will be healed, stopped or make sense some day. Have him give you whatever gift you need. Hold the image as long as you need. His very presence is healing.

Step 8. End the time with a prayer, thanking him for his presence and asking him for direction to guide your needs.

Thought Stopping and Substitution

This exercise, adapted from the work of Joseph Wolpe and Donald

Meichanbaum, is a five-stage process which interrupts and replaces distressing thoughts. This technique is especially helpful in the areas of put-downs, negative labeling, self-talk, critical thoughts and past regrets.

Put-downs or negative labeling will create low self-esteem. Thoughts that imagine the future to be terrible tend to create anxiety. Obsessions about failures and mistakes usually contribute to depression and shame. The more you are obsessed with shame-inducing thoughts, the more shame you will feel. Thought stopping stops this endless merry-go-round.

Step 1. Identify the thought. By now you have knowledge about some thoughts that create distress. If you have not listed any yet, take a moment and list those that come to your mind. Then rank them from the most disturbing to the least. Now choose the one you want to work on using this technique. It might be helpful at first to pick the least disturbing.

Step 2. Imagine the thought. Close your eyes and imagine a situation in which the stressful thought is likely to occur. If you have trouble thinking of a scene, review some of your writing. Find one that fits the thoughts you are working on today. Use your imagination to create as much about the scene as possible: the clothes you have on, the time of day, the sounds, smells, people and feelings that are present. Then let your self-talk just flow naturally. If you begin to feel bad, fear or depressed, your visualization is probably working.

Step 3. Interrupt the thought. At first you may want to set an alarm clock for three minutes. When the alarm goes off, yell, "Stop!" Some have used a tape recorder with the word, "Stop!" recorded at three minutes. Turn the recorder on then sit back and imagine the scene. When the recorder yells, "Stop!" join in with your own yell. Sometimes it is helpful to jump up or clap your hands together.

Step 4. Interrupt the thought without an aid. Now you take control of stopping your thought. Set the timer again, imagine the scene and yell, "Stop!" in three minutes. Then repeat the exercise but set the timer for two minutes. Continue to repeat the exercise but say, "Stop!" in a normal voice. If you have a little trouble here, put a rubber band around your wrist and snap it when you say "Stop!" Continue the exercise eventually saying, "Stop," in a whisper, then silently to yourself. Do not use the recorder anymore. Just confront the thought immediately when you notice it. Again, use a rubber band if you need to. Practice silently confronting the distressing thought as often as you need.

Step 5. Substitute a new thought. After you stop the ineffective thought, the mind will go blank for several seconds. Sometimes, as much as thirty to sixty seconds. It is during this time you will want to replace the old thought with a more effective thought. And the thought needs to be appropriately matched to the thought you are trying to eliminate.

Some examples of replacement thoughts are:

"I am a person of worth."

"Take a deep breath, pause, relax."

"This too shall pass."

"It's OK to be imperfect."

"Feelings are part of being human."

"I am strong and will continue to grow."

"I will trust in God to sustain me."

"One day at a time."

"This is difficult but not overwhelming."

"Let go and let God."

"I can handle anything for a few minutes."

"My worth does not depend on another's opinion."

"I am valuable."

Each of these positive, realistic statements will reduce the shaming and distressing feelings you have.

Remember that our internal messages have been with us for years and were never challenged. We adhere to them strongly. Breaking them will require practice. This is like learning any skill. You may not do it very well at the beginning, but with time and continued effort, you can develop the skill of thought stopping and thought substitution.

Affirmation Scripts

It is simple to learn how to create and use an affirmation script. People who try it are amazed with the results. But I often find a great deal of resistance to the idea. Affirming ourselves is not something we feel comfortable with. I find many clients feel guilty when they say nice things to themselves. This shows just how deeply the shame is buried within us. We cannot talk nicely to ourselves and, yet, we want to feel better and raise our self-esteem. This is a tough paradox.

An affirmation script is a form of reprogramming the old critical and negative judgmental thoughts we use on ourselves. Since most of the opinions we hold about ourselves came from someone else, the new affirmations are the opinions we give ourselves. They are realistic and positive statements about ourselves.

This technique can take a couple of forms. In one, the positive affirmation is written down fifteen to twenty times each day. Each time the statement is written, wait for a spontaneous response. Usually, this response is negative. Then write the affirmation again. Over and over, keep writing the affirming statement. For example:

1. I, (your name), am a person of worth and value.
2. I, (your name), am a person of worth and value.
3. Repeat above statement.

Another form of affirmation script writing is listing a positive realistic script about yourself. This is read out loud each day. Additions to the script are made all along the recovery path. Let me give an example of such an affirmation script:

I, Cheryl, am a person of worth and value.

I, Cheryl, am made up of many strengths and weaknesses.

I, Cheryl, am highly pleasing to others.

I, Cheryl, have the right to say no.

I, Cheryl, have permission to my feelings.

I, Cheryl, am very responsible.

I, Cheryl, am responsible for what I do, think and feel.

I, Cheryl, am imperfect, but willing to learn.

This type of script is read out loud each day. It is not enough to just look over the list after it is written. It should be spoken.

Other suggestions regarding affirmations are:

1. Stick with an affirmation for some time. Try to write it down for two weeks or so.

2. Reserve some time each day to do this exercise of script writing. Plan the time as part of your recovery work.

3. Record your affirmations on a cassette and play them back.

4. Use the technique of visualization in combination with affirmations.

5. Say the statements aloud while looking into a mirror. Become a little dramatic and act out the role of the person you say you are.

6. Use Scripture to build a stronger script. As you look through the Bible, you'll find words that comfort, heal and support you in your journey. I encourage you to memorize key passages that relate to your personal journey. Or put them down on an index card. Then each morning or evening, review the cards.

If the issue you face is abandonment, you may want to use Romans 8:38-39: "For I am convinced that neither death nor life, neither angels nor demons, neither the present nor the future, nor any powers, neither height nor depth, nor anything else in all creation, will be able to separate us from the love of God that is in Christ Jesus our Lord."

If you are trying to build hope because of the chaotic past, Paul addresses the issue in 2 Corinthians 1:8-10: "We were under great pressure, far beyond our ability to endure, so that we despaired even of life. Indeed, in our hearts we felt the sentence of death. But this happened that we might not rely on ourselves but on God, who raises the dead . . . . On him we have set our hope that he will continue to deliver us. . . ."

Both of these are a little lengthy for the affirmation scripting, but I found them useful to read aloud and memorize. I trust you will search out those Scriptures that apply directly to your situation.

Using this technique is like the rest. It takes time and practice to become more efficient at the skill. But the side benefit is better feelings and increased self-worth while you are practicing. Many times bad feelings will come back and you'll find yourself discouraged. But stay with it and the results will begin to show up.

11
BUILDING AWARENESS
OF OUR BEHAVIOR

♦ ♦ ♦

*T*he more I am honest with myself, the more I find I'm not very proud of the way I act. It seems I've spent my life blaming others so much I haven't had time to look at what I do and how my behavior is inappropriate. *Ken*

I'm really wanting to spend more time with my family, but I can't get far enough ahead in my work to free up the weekends or take a trip with them. I'm not as mad at myself as I used to get. But I don't like leaving them alone like my dad did when I was a boy. *Virgil*

So far in this book we have learned to become aware of, accept and take action regarding our feelings and our thoughts. It is now time to apply the

AAA format to the third area—behavior. Like Ken and Virgil, many of the behavior patterns ACAs learned as children continue to create a dysfunctional lifestyle as an adult. ACAs found a way of adapting their behavior, as children, in order to survive the chaos, unpredictability and inconsistency of their home. Many discover they overlearned certain behaviors and underlearned others. It is important to understand that each of us develops a cluster of behavior patterns that we used to survive our childhood chaos but that have overstayed their welcome in our adult life.

Most adult children are prone to extremes. Finding the extremes in each of our lives is part of the task of recovery. By identifying the behavior patterns that we overlearned and overused, we are able to break them. But breaking those patterns requires practice, risk-taking, courage and a faith in God. It is vital for each of us to be connected with a support group, with a 12-step group, a church fellowship, peers who are in recovery, a therapist or a pastor.

Many ACAs feel isolated and disconnected with people around them. It is vital and essential for ACAs to reach out and risk contact with others. This way we can gain support, encouragement and the needed reality checks that help restore sanity to our chaotic existence. The patterns that most of us follow lead us to destruction and are sorely in need of repair. What once helped us to survive no longer is our friend. Behind the behavior patterns we have chosen to help us survive lie dangers and continued pain.

Many times a person will come to me expressing a need to change. Behind their plea for help, however, is a strong resistance to change. It really does seem for most of us the more things we want to change, the more things stay the same. We like to stay in a comfort zone, even if it creates pain and misery. Breaking our behavior patterns can give us a chance to heal, but it is scary and takes a lot of risk.

I look at most behaviors as a person's best attempt to meet the needs that are left over from childhood. I trust that you will take time to examine yourself and to be as honest as you can with yourself. I've said before, the truth will set us free but first it often makes us miserable. It is very difficult for each of us to take a hard look at ourselves and be realistic and honest with our behavior.

A client once told me that he took a hard look at the trail behind him, and he could not count the number of broken relationships, offended friends, failures and "body bags." He wept and felt very sad after taking a hard look at himself. He's no different from you or me. Looking at our behavior and taking responsibility for the way we behave is indeed a sobering and thought-provoking process.

But we really can teach an old dog new tricks. There are a variety of ways that help us find a different way of thinking about the problems we face. Weiss and Weiss, in their book *Recovery from Co-dependency*, say we can address our problem behaviors with the following questions:

1. What do you want to change?
2. What keeps you from making that change?
3. What help, protection or resources do you need in order to make the change?
4. What do you need?
5. What are you going to do to get that need met?

Each of us can look at our own lives, ask ourselves these questions and walk through the changes we want to make.

Childhood Needs That Are Blocked

I know most of you have some sense of the feelings and thought processes within you. As children our needs, wants and feelings were dismissed as unimportant, so we didn't have a normal development process. There are four major discounts that we adopt as children in order to survive.

1. We discount the problem.
2. We discount the significance of the problem.

3. We discount that the problem can be solved.

4. And we discount our feelings and capabilities.

These four discounting strategies are part of our survival mechanism. But it leads us to poorly express what we need as a child. It contributes toward indirectly expressing our needs and wants, and it fosters a passive approach in our personal life. Because we were unable to follow a normal course of development as a child, we still remain very childish in our notions about life, others and ourselves.

Dependency is a normal and vital part of growing up. The development of the child in a functional family would help the child move from dependency through the stages to an interdependency. Because this normal development process is blocked, most adult children are still trying to please their parents and gain the approval they missed as children. This strategy usually fails to meet the needs of significance, approval and validation.

When the needs, wants and feelings of a child are blocked, the child learns substitute behaviors in order to meet the approval and validate needs. These substitute behaviors, when they are at the expense of the child, will ultimately create more destruction for the child.

For example, as a boy, Bob had met with a great deal of disapproval for his angry feelings. When confronted with constant disappointment and broken promises in his family, he was normally agitated and upset. But both his parents could not handle the normal angry feelings Bob tried to express. They would shame him and tell him he was bad for having such feelings.

One day after engaging in a fight with a neighbor boy, Bob was very afraid of coming home. He thought that once again his parents would disapprove of him, be angry at him, yell and send him to his room. What he found startled him. His dad was very proud of him for standing up against the neighbor boy. His mother expressed great pleasure in finally having someone in the neighborhood give those

"Joneses" what they deserved. While he was confused by their reaction, he was nonetheless pleased. His parents liked him and that felt good. Bob's fighting increased and so did his self-esteem. His search for his approval needs from his parents was finally being met.

In high school, however, Bob was suspended for fighting. His parents were embarrassed and angry with him. In the principal's office his dad looked at him and, with an angry body posture, leaned over him and said, "What's wrong with you? You've always been a bully. When will you ever learn?"

His mom looked at him and with disgust in her voice said, "Bob, you're an embarrassment to this whole family. I just can't look at you."

Bob was devastated and felt betrayed. They never understood what all this meant to him. He came to me at the request of his supervisor to deal with the stress of his "angry attitude." Bob was still fighting. Not quite as directly, but still fighting nonetheless. He had trouble getting along with his coworkers and supervisors.

Bob's substitute behavior to feel OK about himself was fighting. Continuing that pattern as an adult often left him frustrated, jobless and rejected by people close to him. They were tired of his constant rage and put-downs. Bob needed to understand his unmet needs. His substitute behavior could not meet those needs. Bob was afraid of being close. He was afraid of rejection.

One day Bob said to me, "All I ever really wanted was for my parents to like me." In his quest for approval he pushed away most of the people in his life that tried to offer approval and closeness to him. As Bob took an honest look at himself and his attempts to control the events and people around him, he was able to view the results and consequences of his behavior. He was able to see that the very needs he had hoped to meet were always outside of his grasp.

Bob is no different from most of us. He overlearned a behavior that provided temporary good feelings about himself. But the price tag in the long run was continued low self-esteem, lack of emotional close-

ness, and a sense of frustration and anger. Each of us needs to examine the patterns that we use that re-create past craziness today.

There are a lot of strengths inherent within the patterns that we use
from our childhood. One way that I define weakness is a strength in
excess. For example, an ability to give of our time and efforts to other
people is a wonderful gift. I call that a strength. However, when that
is the only response available, we will not be able to demonstrate
more assertive behavior when it is required. If I do not meet my own
inner needs, it is a weakness.

A friend of mine I admire always stands up for himself. He's very
assertive about situations that he deems to be wrong. I admire him
for that strength. But I must confess there are times when I view him
as a bit stubborn. He considers himself to be so right that no other
opinion or idea seems to hold water. I view that as a weakness.

Often we're prone to be very critical of our weaknesses and fail to
see that inherent within the weakness is usually a strength in excess.
Part of recovery is learning to establish balance and appropriate
boundaries within ourselves. Discovering a balance that fits us is part
of the process of recovery.

Julie is a Christian who has practiced her faith for over forty years.
One of her rules for living the Christian life is, "Never confront those
in authority over you." In many situations her rule of submitting to
those in authority is wise. But there came a time when Julie had to
see that her rule needed to be amended.

At her church there had been a change in leadership and purpose
and goals over the ten years she attended there. Many of the leaders
she had trusted for years had resigned. In their place were leaders
who seemed more interested in the quantity of numbers attending the
church rather than the quality of spirituality in the church. They
seemed to preach a standard of "whatever you're doing for the Lord
will never be enough." She found herself increasingly discontent with
the policies and decisions made by the leadership.

Being an older person, she was unable to attend many of the church's meetings. After confrontations by her leaders directing her to attend more, regardless of her handicaps, she had to face the fact that perhaps these leaders were not really as wise and as spiritual as she once thought. This was very difficult for her.

Her whole life was led by the idea that one always submits to those in authority, regardless of the position and policy of those in authority. While it is important to submit to those in authority, I would view it as a weakness in need of balance. Especially if the leadership of an organization imposes rules that are inappropriate.

Compulsive Life Patterns

Compulsive life patterns began because as children ACAs adopted behavioral strategies in order to survive the chaos of their troubled home. There are three factors we need to understand about compulsive life patterns. First, we commonly have a mistaken belief that this behavior will lead to achieving our goals. Second, each behavior pattern results in a certain intermittent reward which reinforces the behavior pattern. Third, continuing our survival behavior allows us to avoid painful feelings and problems.

As time progresses and our compulsive life patterns become more a part of us, they create complications psychologically, physically and interpersonally. The irony of this is that by perpetuating our childhood survival behavior patterns, we create unbalanced situations in adult life that need to be survived. Once again we are able to see that we have created the childhood trauma as an adult. Lane Lasater in *Recovery from Compulsive Behavior* found five common patterns in adults. Let's look at each of the five compulsive life patterns and describe the primary behavior and missing skills in each area.

1. Compulsive Working. Compulsive workers work more than fifty hours per week, consider their occupation their primary identity, work when they need to spend time with family or friends, or neglect health or rest because of work. The missing skills are the ability to relax during unstructured time and the capacity to be emotionally close.

2. Relationship Dependency. People who are relationship dependent invest time, energy and affection in a relationship with a person who does not reciprocate equally. They subordinate their own wishes, needs and values to accommodate a partner. They take most or all of the responsibility for problems in a relationship. Or they worry more about the other person's problems than they worry about themselves. The missing skills are the awareness of personal feelings and needs, and the ability to protect oneself from criticism and abuse.

3. Generalized Rebellion. When we experience generalized rebellion, we engage in uninvited attempts to influence people and organizations, frequently take a scapegoat or fall-guy role in situations, take responsibility for things that are not our concern, or use gentle persuasion at first, then turn to more aggressive tactics when others do not respond. The missing skills include the ability to allow issues to pass without challenge and the ability to disengage from people or situations when it becomes apparent that one cannot directly influence them.

4. Victim Syndrome. The victim syndrome is marked by participating naively or passively in situations that affect our well-being, trying to get other people to take care of us, expressing hostility passively or indirectly in relationships, or letting authority figures such as parents, professionals or church authorities tell us what is best to do. The missing skills include the awareness of personal feelings and needs, and the ability to directly assert our own wishes and rights.

5. Perpetual-Child Syndrome. The perpetual-child syndrome is seen in not following through on our commitments, getting others to take care of our own responsibilities, frequently asking that allowances be made for our special circumstances or limitations, or finding that others are often angry because of our behavior. The missing skill is taking responsibility for ourselves.

If you, at this point, find that one of the compulsive life patterns seems to fit for you, then you are following the first step of the AAA recovery format and building awareness about your behavior. It is important to understand that compulsive patterns create more pain for us. It is essential to our recovery to recognize, understand our patterns and find ways to break out of the unproductive compulsive life patterns.

Compulsive Escapes

Compulsive escapes are attempts to comfort ourselves because of our pain. Lasater lists seven escapes:

1. Alcohol, drug and cigarette abuse.
2. Over- and undereating.
3. Compulsive sexual behavior.
4. Compulsive spending.
5. Compulsive religious behavior.
6. Compulsive gambling.
7. Compulsive exercising.

Each of us seeks to change and alter our moods. We can do so by taking a hot shower, going for a walk, watching a beautiful sunset, playing with children, watching our favorite movie, listening to music or attending a church service. The more uncomfortable and upset we feel in life, the more we seek out ways to escape and avoid our pain. Because the relief that we feel in an escape path is immediate, it is powerfully reinforcing to us. The more we are reinforced to avoid our pain through the use of these escapes, the more we desire them. Escapes then become compulsive, and we are unable to stop them.

We feel controlled by them, and we begin to be obsessed about the escapes. The more obsessed we are about our particular escape, the more driven we feel.

Lasater suggests four common phases in the development of compulsive escapes.

1. We make friends with an escape. Once we learn about drinking alcohol or going on spending sprees or taking physical risks, we find that the actions feel good and do not have immediate unacceptable consequences. Therefore we repeat them. Over the years we develop thousands of experiences with those activities that we rely on to provide short-term pain relief for us.

2. Our problems and pain increase. The escape behaviors begin to create new problems for us. We now have two problems. First, the problems that we were using the escapes to avoid, and second, the new complications that our avoidance behaviors have brought to us.

3. We feel remorse over our actions. As we determine that our actions are not really in our best interest and are not consistent with our personal values, our respect is damaged and we feel more shame and less good feelings about ourselves. We usually feel saddened and guilty as we look at our actions. This creates more pain within us. However, regardless of the significant consequences we might face, we feel unable to stop our escape behavior. It is like reaching into our survival tool kit for a strategy to avoid the pain we feel, and we find the same escape behavior we recently used. Even though it does not make sense to use a behavior that is creating pain for us, we have no other alternative in our tool kit.

4. Escaping becomes chronic. As time goes on we give escape strategies our priority for living. In other words, our lifestyle reflects one who is seeking to avoid pain, reduce emotional turmoil and create situations where everything seems OK by escaping. The truth is we develop more guilt and shame, depression and health problems, family conflicts and interpersonal difficulties. We feel out of control and desperate. This usually leads to a crisis point in our escape living where the problems we are trying to flee and the compulsive patterns and escapes we use to flee the pain all collide.

In looking back over the escapes and compulsive life patterns that we use, I think it is very difficult for most of us to really face the truth about ourselves. I would encourage you to make sure that the vicious criticizing voice within you is not tearing you apart. We have to develop an honest look at our behavior, but at the same time, we need to moderate our tendency for attacking ourselves. In the AAA format, acceptance is needed when we look clearly at our behavior. We need to accept the behavior as real, and accept ourselves as imperfect adults.

Since these strategies have rarely been recognized as attempts to meet inner needs, it is important for ACAs to counter perfectionistic self-criticism. We are responsible for ourselves. It is our behavior. No one makes us do what we do.

To recognize, uncover and deal honestly with ourselves takes courage. We need to practice comfort strategies or the worst happens again. We re-enact the shame and criticizing cycle that we had as children. And that is just the reason so many of the behavior patterns and escapes are deeply entrenched within us. They were a way of adapting, surviving and helping us to feel good about ourselves.

Whatever you are beginning to build awareness about, take heart. Others have also felt discouraged and defeated as they looked at their patterns. Keep coming back. Change is possible. Recovery is possible. Adapting the worn-out compulsive patterns is possible. In the following chapter we will look at some strategies that promote change, but here our focus has been on building awareness.

It is important to anchor down the particular patterns that you want to change. Take a minute and write out the key areas you are discovering about yourself that you would like to adapt. Then take time to nourish and be gentle with the tender person within you.

I once attended a conference where midway through the presentation the lecturer stopped, looked across the audience, and asked one question. "What would it be like for each of you to live without the crisis and high stress that you've become accustomed to?"

There were some snickers throughout the audience. One of the participants raised his hand and was acknowledged by the lecturer. The participant responded with, "I don't know what it'll be like, but I sure hope it gets here soon." We all laughed. But the truth of that participant's statement rang in my ears. <u>Most</u> adult children <u>do not know any other way of living than</u> that of chaos and crisis. They do not want the pain and misery they feel, but in all honesty, do not know how to change. I guess I would ask myself and you the same question. "What would today look like for me to live without all of the crisis and stress I've become so accustomed to?" And making that even more practical, "What is one part of today I would really like to change in order to create less stress in my own recovery journey?"

To answer this question I would go back to the questions listed earlier in this chapter. What is it I want to change and what stands in the way that blocks me from that change? I must admit, the real enemy of my change is me.

In my own recovery trail, I have not liked what I discovered about myself. I have not liked what I discovered happened to me as a child. I have not liked the patterns of behavior I used to escape my pain. I must admit that when it came time to begin change within me, there was no longer my parents or my circumstances to inhibit me. It was me. Yes, it was my fear, my lack of trust, my own <u>inability to take risks</u> that held me back. It was the behaviors I had overlearned. Now those behaviors were like a poisonous snake returning to bite me and hurt me and poison me.

In building awareness about our patterns I encourage you to go slowly and build upon the earlier framework we've learned. You see, even now you need to give yourself credit for being on a journey and for having taken steps to stay on that journey. The action steps in early recovery are not intended to build a whole new you. The steps are intended to build awareness about the person you are and what has happened to you. They help you discover your strengths and admit your powerlessness. They cause you to turn yourself over to God and build a support group.

Awareness-Building Tips

Let me summarize a few ideas you may find useful in building aware
ness. Don't feel as though you have to do them all. Try out one or
more of these tips that you think would be most helpful for you.

1. Keep a journal.
2. Ask yourself the questions I have listed on page 129 in this
chapter.
3. Record every day a reality snapshot.
4. Join a support group, and talk with others in recovery.
5. Gather more information by reading or attending workshops.
6. Join an ACA or codependency therapy group.
7. Seek out a therapist or pastor.
8. Talk with the significant people in your life. Listen to their
observations about you.
9. Ask yourself what you want to stop doing and what you want to
start doing.

Over my years of recovery I have discovered that happiness is a by-
product. It is not what we pursue. It is a by-product of taking good care
of ourselves, of developing strategies that enhance the person we are,
and of learning different ways of resolving the collision between others' needs and our needs.

Paul said in Philippians that he learned to live with contentment
in want and in plenty. We can have contentment by living with integ-
rity, taking responsibility for ourselves and treating ourselves and
others with respect.

12
CHANGING
OUR BEHAVIOR
♦ ♦ ♦

I have been to several groups, and I feel good about the aware-ness I have built about my life, my family of origin and the feelings I have. But one thing bothers me. I keep doing the same things over and over. Before I didn't know what was going on inside of me. Now I do. I guess it is good that I'm breaking through denial. But I keep repeating the same behaviors. Only now I'm really aware of the way I act. And I have to tell you, I don't feel good about it. I don't want to stop my recovery path, but I am not sure that it is making a lot of difference in my life right now. I'm pretty good about talking and going to my support groups when I feel angry and upset. But I just talk, talk, talk and then act the same way. I want to change and get better. It just feels like I'm stuck or at a plateau. *Gordon*

The need to identify and change behavior patterns is as important to the healing process as other skills. Since the process of developing the ineffective patterns of thinking, feeling and behaving is made up of thousands of experiences, the regenerating process will be very similar. Each time we can re-experience life in a more healthy manner, we slowly rebuild the way we view life and the way we react to life.

The parents and significant people are responsible for the toxic environment children were raised in, not the children. But as adults, ACAs are responsible for the style of life they continue to create for themselves. As adults, they have taken over the job of running their lives. How it is run, and the quality of living is now up to them. While it is true they do not have the skills others were given in their family of origin, as adults they can begin the building process.

Remember, in your family of origin you learned most every rule, perception, evaluation and behavior pattern. Each of us can unlearn those that do not work and relearn more effective patterns.

The spiritual part of the healing journey is so essential because the basis of Scripture is hope—hope that we can change and be transformed, hope that there is a Comforter who was sent to help us, hope that we will never be abandoned, hope that no matter what the problem, change is possible.

All of us are changed like the caterpillar into a butterfly. The old passes away and the new is brought into life. The old inner person is regenerated by the work of God into a new creation. Sometimes, the recovery path is slow and difficult. Without hope, the tendency is to give up. Hope continues to propel us forward into the next day's recovery.

In the well-used slogan of AA, we continue to "Let Go and Let God." But, without a sustained and clear recovery path, hope fades. When we see the futility of our existence and the continued ineffective patterns, we get discouraged and defeated. Hope sustains us while we rebuild our broken lives. Then, as we observe God's faithfulness and witness positive consequences from our effective behaviors, we gather evidence that change is possible and probable.

Adult children are raised in such a manner that problem solving is rarely taught, conflict is avoided, and behavior becomes very rigid and repetitive. In addition, questioning parents or the decisions they make is taboo, risk taking is not encouraged, and problems in the family are opportunities for blame. Given this scenario it is no wonder that adult children have an unhealthy style for problem solving.

Principles for Changing Behavior

When a need arises for changing behavior, adult children are either frozen and paralyzed, or compulsively act out some escape behavior. Either way, the creativity needed to see another option is absent and the risk-taking ability needed to act on the creative option is missing. This chapter presents a systematic approach you can use as you decide on the patterns you want to change.

Principle #1: Awareness. The AAA format for changing our thoughts and feelings starts with awareness. The same is true for changing our behavior. We need to fully understand the patterns that we wish to change. This is similar to step one in the 12-step recovery program. It is coming to awareness about the behavior, the consequences and the reasons you continue to live the way you do. Chapter eleven may be helpful in examining the patterns. Whatever you use to build an honest look at yourself, you decide. But when you fail to take an honest, truthful look, denial is still in charge. Take the time to really examine your behavior and the consequences. It is vital for you to be specific about the behaviors you want to change.

Principle #2: Specific Goals. The goals you want to attain need to be identified and broken down into manageable steps. Often ACAs fail because their goals are too general. I use the notion of changing a "little bit." By giving attention to a specific area, the probability of success increases dramatically. For instance, if a person needs to deal with a long-standing alcohol problem, other issues need to be delayed as the individual builds a strong program of recovery from alcohol.

The steps need to be small in order to create clear behavior targets. One ACA commented, "I want to have a closer relationship with God." The specific daily steps were prayer time, reading in the Bible, going to church services and setting up weekly meetings with the pastor.

Short-range goals are essential to achieving long-range goals. What we choose within each day provides the foundation for tomorrow. What we sow, we reap. The harvest of life is made up of the seeds we plant today.

Principle #3: Stopping Ineffective Behavior. The plan for stopping the ineffective behaviors has to be clear. If we do not identify clearly the people, places and events that have maintained the behavior, we will have trouble stopping it.

Write on a sheet of paper the people who continue to encourage the behavior, the places where you normally produce the behavior and the events that stimulate the behavior. Once the list is gathered make decisions about the information. Avoid the people, places and events that promote your high-risk behavior. Plan to go to new places. Rebuild a network of people who are honest, truth seeking and in recovery. Plan new events for the times that are difficult. Develop a phone of supportive people.

For example, Fred, a deacon in a local church, clearly identified his escape from pressure. He would go to topless dancing bars. After he would spend the evening there, he would feel guilt, shame and remorse. He would vow to "never let it happen again" on his drive home. When he would arrive home, he could not face his wife. She was upset because he was late. He would get angry with her, and then they would argue. The night would end in silence, isolation and both felt emotionally distant.

So Fred made a plan. He said, "When I feel pressured and entertain the idea of going to a topless bar, I will use thought stopping to fight the thoughts. I will call my wife and talk with her about my feelings. [He had previously confessed his compulsive escape, and the two of them committed to a recovery program together.] I will commit to drive straight home. I will take time once I'm home to relax, talk with my wife, pray together and go for a walk. Later, I will try to discover what is pressuring me and what decisions I need to make to confront the situation."

While there are other strategies Fred could have used, this plan worked for him. In time he did deal with the identity issues, intimacy issues and fear of trust within himself. But it was imperative that he stop the compulsive escape and that he have a clear plan to accomplish his desired goal.

Principle #4: Challenge Ineffective Thinking. The thoughts that maintain the old patterns need to be identified, challenged and more appropriate messages put in place. I have already mentioned many thinking patterns that create distressful and destructive behavior patterns. Suffice it to say, much of what we do to ourselves is "stinkin'-thinkin.' " Fred fought with the messages which said, "Just one more time," "This won't hurt anyone," and "I deserve this trip." There were more, but those three were key ideas that he used to justify his behavior. As he confronted them and focused his attention on his wife and his commitments, he would get home without an escape.

Principle #5: Reinforce New Patterns. Devise reinforcement strategies for the new thinking and behavior patterns. It is a true statement that "behavior that is reinforced is increased and maintained."

The payoff for behavior will determine how long it is sustained. Most adult children are unaware how their behavior is being reinforced by themselves and others. When new patterns are chosen, thought needs to be given to the specific manner the behaviors will be reinforced. Reinforcement is the immediate consequence a person receives after a behavior.

While avoiding a stressful situation may ultimately fail to address the needs of the situation, the feeling of short-term relief is strong enough to maintain the avoiding behavior. When a person drinks to escape painful emotions, the mood of a person is altered. Drinking is reinforced because the alcohol changes the emotional state of the person. At the time it does not seem to matter to the person that he or she will be more depressed later.

For a compulsive shopper, buying brings pleasure. For a while good feelings of self-esteem exist. The crash comes later when the bill comes or the money is not there to buy necessities or the shopper lies about the purchases to his or her spouse. All of these behaviors are maintained because they are being reinforced.

As you decide on new behaviors, plan appropriate reinforcement strategies to increase the behavior. Reinforcement can come from several sources.

☐ Self-Talk. Say to yourself things like, "I did a good job." "I'm proud of you for choosing the healthy path." "Keep up the good work. It will help your depression." "Keep taking little steps because they all add up." "I can do it." "I value and respect myself for choosing wellness."

☐ Pleasant Activities. You can reward yourself by getting a massage, going to the hot tub, watching a favorite TV show, going fishing, going to a play or movie, playing basketball, reading a novel or doing something else very comforting.

☐ Tokens. A useful reinforcement program for children is giving them a token after each behavior. They can accumulate them and redeem them for larger prizes or awards. As adults you can do the same thing by establishing that a certain number of tokens will be redeemed for a specific activity. Giving yourself a token when you produce the behavior you want encourages you to continue the behavior. You could redeem them for an activity described in the previous paragraph or anything else you choose.

☐ Participation by Others. Involving others in the reinforcement of appropriate behavior is powerful. Of course, this assumes you have talked with the significant people and they agree to the plan. They can praise and encourage you. Ask for what you want from them and how you want the praise delivered to you. Cards, notes, letter of appreciation, back rubs, walks in the park, a favorite meal or dessert, doing some of your chores, giving a night off, a weekend together away—fully supporting an activity even if it means some sacrifice of time.

By having those close to you supporting your behavior change, accountability is increased and you will feel close to the person who is encouraging your changes. I will cover some useful strategies couples can use in the next chapter.

Principle #6: Written Contract. Desired changes need to be written. I believe writing out the behaviors you want to change helps to clarify the contract you make with yourself. In the contract you can state the goal, the means of reinforcement, the method of recording it and the timing for re-evaluation.

An example is Gordon. He was increasing time spent with his family and cutting down extensive work patterns. His contract said, "I agree to stop working at 5:00 on Tuesday and Friday and go home for a dinner with the whole family. Susan and I will monitor my behavior and record it in my spiral binder. The reward for completing this assignment is a choice of the following:

A. Having Susan give me a back rub.

B. Receive one token per night. (Two tokens are needed to attend a basketball game.)

C. Attend a movie with Susan over the weekend.

This contract can be renegotiated in two weeks and new homework added.

Signature _____

Signature _____

Principle #7: Commit to Make Decisions. I think it is clear by now that no one can decide for you what behaviors you choose to work on. This chapter is based on the premise you are responsible for yourself. You can gather information forever and still not decide to change. You can hide, run, deny, pretend and blame. Still, if nothing changes, nothing changes.

If you are like most people, and I believe you are, you are going to change when you choose to do so. When there is enough pain or destructive living, you will want something different for your life. The truth is, without pain most of us would change very little. Why should we? Pain is often the prime motivator for most people to change, adapt, confront and seek new ways to live. Pain comes in many forms and screams for a remedy. Only you will be the one who ultimately, on bended knee, seeks for a more healthy style of life.

I want to encourage you to make decisions and avoid the trap of just collecting information. We will never know it all, comprehend everything or analyze every situation fully. We need to take whatever steps we can, as soon as we can.

When you do change, you may be surprised to find yourself grieving. All of the decisions you make to change behaviors will result in loss and sadness. Every decision for one behavior is a decision against another. Giving up our habits and old patterns is similar to letting go of an old friend. Many ACAs relapse because they forget to work on the emotional side of recovery.

All of the strategies to change behaviors cannot ever replace the fact ACAs will have to feel their pain, experience healing and walk through the hurts. Too often we are promised a simple and quick solution to healing where none exists.

True healing comes from the inside. No new rules for behaving can ever replace the continued recovery work we need in order to restore our wounded feelings and rebuild our fractured sense of personhood.

Daily Recovery Program

Recovery is taken one day at a time. Therefore, it is vital for you to develop a daily program of behavior change. The recovery tasks you can choose from are numerous. It is important to decide what you are going to focus on for the day. The small steps you take will add up over time, and you will notice changes in thinking, feeling and behavior. By now you have some notions about the areas you want to change. By building a recovery program around those areas your healing path will be more focused.

In the closing chapter, I have listed several recovery areas you may choose to focus on in building your recovery program. In this section I want to present a few ideas to help explain the daily recovery program. If one fits for you, take it and try it out.

The first one I like to call Taking Care of Business, or TCOB. I used it for years in my recovery journey. Look at figure 4. Each category has specific tasks. For instance, a sample of tasks is: Spiritual—prayer time; Emotional—write about my feelings; Physical—walk one mile. I would check off the day I accomplished the task. My goal was to

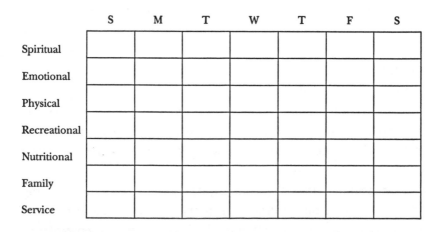

	S	M	T	W	T	F	S
Spiritual							
Emotional							
Physical							
Recreational							
Nutritional							
Family							
Service							

Figure 4. *Taking Care of Business (TCOB) Chart*

complete as many as I could each day. As the tasks became a new habit, I would add others. Or I would change the task as I discovered more appropriate recovery needs. You can make any list of categories that fit your recovery journey.

Another way is to start the day with a theme for the day. For instance, you might have as a theme "God's Faithfulness." Then, throughout the day you would stop, pause and reflect upon the theme. At the end of the day, you would write about what you learned, what applied to you and what decisions you need to make. Sometimes, the themes will carry on for days. You add a theme whenever you are ready. Sometimes, you will discontinue a theme and pick it up again later.

I found the following recovery guide from an alcohol- and chemical-dependency program at St. Vincent's Hospital in Portland, Oregon. It reflects the ideas of a focused, daily format for recovery. It's found in figure 5. You can easily see why it's called R & R.

Another method some have found effective is the use of a workbook written for adult children. Some are written in a 12-step format. All of them blend recovery concepts with numerous exercises the reader actively participates in as the book is read. The workbook can be used individually or concurrently with support groups, group therapy or individual therapy. A few of the workbooks are:

The Twelve Steps—A Spiritual Journey Based on Biblical Teachings
Repeat after Me by Claudia Black
A Gentle Path through the Twelve Steps by Patrick Carnes
A Workbook for Healing by Patty McConnell
A Gift to Myself by Charles L. Whitfield

There are numerous approaches to a daily program of recovery. Find what works for you and repeat it often. My desire is to encourage you to take seriously the need to develop a daily program. Keep the program simple and focused.

Behavior change is possible and healing is possible. However, the

When Tempted to Drink or Use Drugs—Remember to Use R & R

1. Relax
It requires all of your emotional strength to fight chemical dependency. Use physical exercise, deep breathing, meditation or another relaxation technique to relieve stress or emotional tension. Most relapses occur after an emotional upset, an argument with a loved one, or social pressures.

2. Reward
Set goals for yourself and plan rewards if you succeed. The reward can be small or large, but it probably should not be food. Rewarding yourself with rich desserts and banana splits could end in another battle—losing weight or mood swings. Learn to enjoy simple pleasures.

3. Remember
You may lose sight of the reasons you wanted to kick your habit. As you start, make a list of those features that upset you most about drinking/drugs such as a bad example for your children, and refer to it at your low points. Remember, you had the will power to try to quit (which is more than many users can say) and you have already made it through the toughest hours.

4. Resist
When you have the urge to use, try to wait ten minutes before doing it. In that time, think about why you want to quit, focus on how much better you will feel when you stop, and remember how strong you have been so far.

5. Replace
Substitute bad habits with good ones. Drink plenty of water, juice and decaffeinated beverages. Eat regular and healthy meals. Get daily exercise. Stick with your friends and family who are "winners."

6. Resolve
You may have a few setbacks in the first few weeks. Do not label yourself as weak or without will power and settle back into full-fledged drinking or drug use. Keep an eye on your final goal and remember how many times you have successfully resisted the urge to use. Two (or ten) slips on the way to that goal do not make you a failure. Stopping the effort entirely is the only failure. Learn from the past, but look to the future.

Figure 5. *R & R*   Taken from the *R. & R. Guide* and used by permission of the author.

steps take risk and any movement is uncomfortable. The alternative is to remain the same and continue with the pain you have had for years. We can take the fear we have to change and convert it to an energy that promotes risk taking. Remember to build a network of supportive people that will enhance your recovery efforts. Include those people who believe in health and protect yourself from those that are toxic.

I leave you with a poem by an unknown author.

One day I found a brand new me
Which some of my friends couldn't see.
He was every bit as real a guy
As the more familiar I,
But with an unfamiliar script
Which told them surely I had flipped. . . .
They thought that who we really are
Was only who we'd been so far.
I must say it was a shock
To find these friends a stumbling block.
Along the way to all the me's,
I hope will put my mind at ease.
I wasn't trying to scare or dare
Or show myself as more aware,
But merely trying to share my thoughts
And clear the air, of shoulds and oughts . . .
I never thought they'd find it strange
That I might ever want to change,
'Cause change was something we all knew;
It was just the way you grew.
It seems that staying just the same
Is really just a hopeless game.
It's hard to show that you're for real,
Instead of feeling what you feel,
Instead of following our hearts,
We check ourselves and play the parts.
So I must learn to stay alone
And appreciate this new me on my own,
Until he's such a part of me,
He's something anyone can see.

As you take the steps needed to make the changes you desire, be gentle with yourself, but be disciplined in your behavior. On this day there are countless people just like you resolving to live in a manner that is less destructive and more effective. They too want to live in a style that is more forgiving and less controlling. You are not alone in your quest. Keep on having faith and a spirit of courage. Healing our hearts and living more effectively is possible.

13
RECOVERING
RELATIONSHIPS
♦ ♦ ♦

*I*f I am not for me,
Who will be?
If I am only for me,
What's the purpose?
If not now, when?
Rabbi Hillel

Therefore, as God's chosen people, holy and dearly loved, clothe yourselves with compassion, kindness, humility, gentleness and patience. Bear with each other and forgive whatever grievances you may have against one another. *Colossians 3:12-13*

*F*or me it was like being with people who would hurt me and then make fun of my crying and pouting. But it wasn't just me that would get hurt. I would watch Mom get hit and yelled at and I would be very scared. At night I would be ashamed of the fighting. Sometimes I pretended to be in the neighbors' house. It was the "people next door" that were fighting. Mom and Dad were really asleep and I would get up in the morning and everything would be OK. It was the only way I could sleep. Besides, when I would get up everything was okay. No one talked about what happened the night before. I was scared to bring it up so I didn't. I would just get ready for school and leave as quickly as I could. I wanted to leave before Dad got up. Sometimes I had trouble eating breakfast. I thought at the time that I just didn't eat breakfast. Now I know it's because I was too tight and upset to sit down and eat. I guess I learned to avoid any fighting. It is too uncomfortable for me. Even today if someone speaks harshly with me, I don't eat and sleep very well.   *Bob, a forty-seven-year-old ACA*

Most ACAs have trouble in relationships. They continue to try to find the love and acceptance they missed in childhood. Yet, the skills ACAs have for building relationships fail to capture the closeness they desire. Admittedly, the topic of building relationships at home is too broad to treat fully in one chapter, but in this, the last of three chapters dealing with behaviors, we'll consider some creative steps you can take to enable your relationships to grow and heal.

Bob and Debbie
The relationship of a committed and caring couple has tremendous power to heal both of the partners. A couple can bring out the best or the worst within each person. Bob was raised in a home of physical and emotional abuse. He was filled with terror and was scared. He lived in a war zone. He learned to pretend that his family was OK.

He learned to split off from his feelings and the trauma of his family. He had trouble eating and sleeping. He learned to avoid confrontation. When people fought, he felt out of control just as he did as a child.

Debbie, an ACA, lived with an alcoholic father. He was absent a lot. She felt abandoned most of her life. She would hide as she heard her parents fight about her dad's lack of involvement with the family.

Bob and Debbie have tried on numerous occasions to talk about his work patterns. The following discussion starts at 9:30 P.M., after Bob worked late at the office.

Debbie: It's almost ten. Here's your dinner, cold as usual. What is so important that you just *had* to work late tonight? I'm sick and tired of being second to what you want. You do not care about anyone but yourself. I might as well not be here. You could hire out what I do for you. And do not look at me with those hurt-look eyes. Just saying you're sorry is not enough. If you really cared for me, you would do something about it.

Bob: I'm not hungry right now. Can't we discuss this in the morning? I've worked hard all day. You make it sound like I work all the time, and I don't. I know I should spend a little more time here, and I will. As soon as this project is done, I'll have more time. Can't this wait? It's so late. Well, whatever.

And this is followed with silence by Bob. Debbie continues to talk but Bob is no longer listening. She continues talking up to an hour trying to get him to respond and ends the conversation with, "What good does it do to talk with you? You act like you aren't there." They end the conversation by going to bed.

Bob feels numb and replays in his mind the activities he has planned for the next day. He falls to sleep and wakes up the next morning early. Skipping breakfast, he hurries off to work so he can get his work done sooner and return a little earlier that evening.

Debbie feels anger and resentment. But she also feels guilty after reviewing the argument in her mind. She sleeps poorly, awakes early and does not mention what happened the night before. The day is spent feeling blue and alone.

What is really happening with Bob and Debbie? Yes, an issue that is important to Debbie was raised. But the interaction between the two of them is of vital concern. For Bob, he was immediately feeling just like he did as a child when fighting would start in his family. For him, the issue is more than staying late at the office. He feels attacked, shamed and bad. He is once again scared and feels "icky" about himself. He meets these feelings with his defense mechanism of denial and blocking.

Bob learned to get more validation for himself through his work outside the home. He has developed a lifestyle of compulsive working. He cannot understand why Debbie is so angry. He does not feel safe around anger. He handles conflict today just as he did as a child. He avoids, does not eat, dreams about other things so he can sleep, leaves early for work to avoid more conflict and carries around a knot of fear in his body. He works hard to feel some sense of control, but dreads another confrontation with his wife.

For Debbie, she was re-enacting a familiar scene from her childhood. She was attempting to control Bob's behavior. She did not like the way she felt after her attacks on Bob, but it seemed to be the only way she knew to try to change him. She was not aware that she was dealing with the emptiness, abandonment and loneliness she experienced in her family. The issues of importance, significance and belonging were at stake in the discussion.

After her attempts to control Bob, she would push down her feelings and not raise the issue for some time. Days or weeks would pass without her mentioning to Bob the problems she had about their marriage. She would go through the days completing her duties in the family. Bob originally sought help for "stress" because Debbie said he needed help. Over time Bob's ability to deny and avoid just did not work as well as it once did. He would have angry outbursts. He wanted a divorce because he just "couldn't please Debbie." I concurred that a divorce would be a healthy choice for him. But the divorce I suggested he needed was from a family system he continued to live in as an adult, not a divorce from his wife.

Bob loved his wife but just could not get close. He wanted to feel happy and at peace, but that never seemed to happen at home. His place of relief was outside the home at work. He could feel good about himself and have a sense of mastery that he did not feel at home.

Both Bob and Debbie became committed to healing themselves and their relationship. The gains were slow but because both were involved in the recovery process, their relationship became a source of healing instead of pain.

Much of this book is written for individual healing; however, one does not heal alone. Our primary relationships need repair work in order to provide safety for each person to grow. I believe there is an incredible power waiting to be tapped within the primary relationship.

I received a card from Bob some time back. It had been months since our last session together. On the front of the card was a little boy with large ears, big eyes, a huge smile and torn clothes. The little boy was dancing or jumping up and down. I opened the card and found these words:

Ears to hear what is really being said,
Eyes to see what is really happening,
Permission to love and just be me,
Makes me dance and smile with glee.

Characteristics That Affect Relationships

What are some of the common traits of relationships that ACAs have with others? Let's look at a few.

Crisis-oriented Living. Some adult children seem to exist in a state of crisis most of the time. They seek out situations that are complex and nonproductive. They involve themselves in relationships where it is almost impossible to feel good about themselves. ACAs feel a sense of discomfort when life is calm. They are constantly waiting for something to go wrong.

I've heard ACAs comment many times, "If there isn't excitement, I feel bored and lose interest." But most adult children have a poor definition of excitement. What they really mean is stress. Since adult children tend to re-create the environment of trauma and involve themselves in situations much like their family of origin, stressful living will always feel most natural—even if the stress is re-enacting the childhood trauma.

Manipulative Behavior. Adult children learned in their family to be indirect and deceptive in order to get needs met. It was not OK to ask for what one wanted, to discuss feelings or to have needs met by the parents. ACAs did not learn creative, constructive options. What is often learned is how to manipulate others. Often, lying becomes such a way of life that the adult child lies about something when telling the truth would have been much easier.

Because they are terrified of making mistakes, being found out or hurting someone's feelings, they often conclude the only way to get what one wants is to deceive and lie. Adult children lie to themselves the most. They have learned from their parents to distort reality. And they continue throughout life distorting reality until as adults they are not sure what is truth and what is not. Many adult children tell me that they live two lives. One life is what they show to others when they pretend. The other is the life they live in secret.

Inability to Have Fun. In a war zone, life is very serious. And in the home where trauma lives, life is without much fun. This causes some adult children to become overly serious. Their life is a constant battle with little humor. At the other extreme are the ones that become clowns to relieve tension in the family and get the attention away from the real problems. Either way the behavior is protective and attempts to avoid the underlying issues of pain and trauma. To those who really do not have fun, planning a party is difficult. There always exists the fear of something going wrong or that it won't turn out perfectly and that they will be blamed. So life becomes void of simple pleasures and the little moments of laughter that honestly do break the tension of living in a tough world. As one is in recovery, learning to laugh, play, have fun and enjoy life becomes a mark of healing.

Attempts to Fit In. Adult children spend so much energy trying to fit in with the crowd. The lack of feeling accepted in the family of origin drives the adult child to try to belong. We guard what we say, how we look, how we act and the choices we make so we always fit. But we still do not feel like we belong. So we try harder. Or we go to the other extreme and act as if it does not even matter if we belong. We seem to not care what anyone says, even those close to us. Either way we are trying, in vain, to have our broken sense of belonging resolved.

People-pleasing. Many adult children try to please everyone around them. It seems like there is no ability to say no. Whatever anyone else wants takes precedence over my needs.

I remember one Saturday I had agreed to help move three different families all on the same day. Instead of realizing my error and letting at least one family know (I could not let two of the three down, you understand) I started at 6:00 in the morning and worked until midnight to the point of exhaustion. Well, at least, that day was over. But I had already agreed to cover for another manager at work on Sunday, so it was off to work after a short night's rest. This is a compulsive way to live. Eventually I suffer the real loss. (Oh, and by the way, when *I* moved, I could not ask for any help. I did not want to inconvenience anyone.)

People-pleasing is full of traps, but the worst trap is that I do not take care of myself in a balanced manner. Fear of rejection and what other people might think motivates adult children to become people-pleasers. It is the excessive nature of the compulsive pleasing that becomes unhealthy. When the only response I have in every situation is pleasing others, I will suffer from the stress of living out of balance.

Poor Boundaries. ACAs have difficulty setting functional boundaries. The family either promoted no separateness and autonomy for the members, or it promoted only separateness and a lack of cohesion.

Boundaries are like an invisible "fence" between people. They serve to protect us from others. They are also our sense of self—our thoughts, feelings, beliefs, goals and behavior. Developing a healthy boundary means fully understanding how we are different from others, taking responsibility for our thoughts, feelings and behavior. If we have healthy boundaries we stop assuming responsibility for what others think, feel and do.

Healthy boundaries must be taught in the family. Usually ACAs are raised in a home where their boundaries are intruded. They develop a poor sense of boundaries. Some have very rigid boundaries—no one can get in and no one can see the real self. Others develop nonexistent boundaries—anyone can intrude since there is no protection. This lack of functional boundaries seriously confuses the marital relationship.

Passive Behavior. Some ACAs seek out crisis and stress. Others are passive. They are afraid to risk and take responsibility for themselves. They wait for others to make decisions for them. Crippled by a fear of failure and rejection, they stand frozen as life faces them.

In relationships, passive ACAs do not step forward and address the issues needed to develop a healthy relationship. In contrast, many ACAs that are passive in their emotional relationships may be quite energetic and risk-taking in the professional arena. This is quite normal for ACAs who were raised as the hero children in their families. Success is essential to well-being, and the business world tends to give better standards to measure success. Although this split between the emotional life and professional life is common, it is very confusing to the other partner in a relationship.

Outer-directed. Developmentally, children will learn the values of the family and internalize them. Over time children need to think independently and understand their values. Then the beliefs about life can become an essential part of them.

In families where trauma and chaos exist, many children only develop the capacity to see the world as the parents see it. This is especially true where a child has heard continual put-downs and criticisms. Who I am as a person is solely defined by others around me. I look to others to let me know whether I am loveable or worthwhile. Part of the recovery process is taking back the style of being more inner-directed rather than solely outer-directed. This is a very difficult process, but the rewards of health and inner peace far outweigh the initial pain of the journey.

Intimacy Problems. Since most adult children did not have a functional, healthy marriage relationship modeled for them, it is rare that they are able to develop healthy relationships for themselves. They tend to be overresponsible or underresponsible in relationships. They are so fearful of abandonment and rejection that really getting close to other people terrifies them.

So they spend a great deal of time moving close then moving apart. It is classically illustrated by the double-message "Come close; stay away." With lots of unfinished business from their own parents, adult children are never really sure whether they are responding to their partner or their parents.

Adult children tend to seek out a mate who matches the negative parental relationship they had as a child. It is as if they are trying once again to gain the acceptance, love and sense of belonging that was not available to them in their family of origin. But such relationships are doomed to chaos because the partners they picked already represent the unfinished business ACAs have with their parents.

Is it any wonder that a high percentage of adult children from alcoholic homes marry alcoholics or become alcoholics themselves?

Or that adults from traumatic, rigid and critical homes marry partners that are critical and abusive?

The greatest gift you bring to any relationship is your personal recovery. The greatest gift a couple will give to each other is a commitment together to a recovery process.

Recovery Principles for Relationships

This closing section builds upon the individual recovery guidelines I've already presented. However, I believe ACAs in recovery can enhance their primary relationship with a few simple tasks. These tasks are simple to explain but are difficult to carry out because the style ACAs use in relationships are deeply ingrained. Certainly a more comprehensive look at building healthy relationships is needed, but for our purposes some early recovery tasks can begin the process of healing the primary relationship.

Principle of Time. The concept of quality versus quantity time has been mentioned in many popular books. No doubt the quality of time couples spend together is important. However, the couple in recovery needs to be prepared for spending time and effort on their relationship. Both partners will need to decide upon the importance of giving extra time to the recovery tasks the relationship requires.

Principle of Risk. To build trust, there is no substitute for taking risks in the relationship. No amount of knowledge can replace the resolve to act differently. Risking takes courage. But like most issues in a relationship, risking becomes reciprocal. That is, as one risks to live in a responsible fashion, speaking honestly and seeking the good of the relationship, it is usually given back by the partner.

Principle of Unmet Needs. Both partners need to understand that each is trying to meet the unmet childhood needs brought to the relationship. As each learns the key issues of the other, strategies can be planned for healing the unmet needs. In the case of Bob and Debbie, Bob began to convey to Debbie how important she was to him, and

Debbie learned to respect Bob for the ways he tried to please Debbie.

ACAs' basic needs of safety, significance, belonging, love and competency are still waiting to be met. Genesis 2:24 says, "For this reason a man will leave his father and mother and be united to his wife." Instead of staying bonded with the parents and their lack of approval, the adult bonds with the spouse and re-establishes a relationship based on meeting the love needs of *both* partners.

Principle of Interruption. I believe most couples can improve their relationships by 100% if they stop doing the things that do not work. Think back over a common issue you have argued about often. Does the conversation have a predictable sense to it? Do you not know with a reasonable certainty just how each of you will talk and how the dispute will end? By interrupting your worn-out patterns, you at least stop some of the constant hurt done in the interaction.

I remember one couple that constantly fought about the laundry. After the usual insults and anger the fight would end, like always, with no resolution and hurt feelings. One day the issue was raised and the husband, trying to follow his goal of not insulting, just reached down into the pile of clean laundry and put on his wife's brassiere. While she was annoyed at first, she soon began to laugh at this grown business executive discussing life while wearing a bra. Later, she did talk with him about her tender feelings and what she really wanted from him. For the first time he heard her pain and not her attack on him.

While I do not recommend their particular interrupting style, it certainly worked for them. For most, you will need to take a time-out, get up and go for a walk together, leave the room you are in and go to the kitchen table, or sit on a couch facing each other.

Principle of Self-responsibility. To recover relationships we must resolve to take personal responsibility for our thoughts, feelings and actions. Conversations between spouses change when one assumes full ownership of his or her feelings and actions instead of blaming others. It enables the couple to gain more understanding of each other rather than shaming, controlling and manipulating their loved one.

Principle of We-ness. Couples need to realize that they are in a battle together. Instead of the war being waged between them, they need to learn to become allies together against the forces that seek to destroy their marriage. Our culture, family messages and destructive style all seek to tear our primary relationship apart. Even the mental-health field gives so many constant messages of separateness, one could conclude that there are not *any* marriages that will work.

The couple has to resolve to both wear the same uniform. Instead of a civil war where one wears blue and the other gray, both need to unite on the same side. There are no bad guys or good guys, just two people who are learning more effective ways to live together.

Principle of Fun. Often couples leave behind the activities they used in dating to get close to each other. As a relationship breaks down, one of the first areas to be forsaken is recreation. I encourage couples to schedule dinners together, plan activities out for the two of them, go away for the weekend, go to the park, the zoo, movies or the theater. It is important to add whatever they would like to increase in their relationship.

Principle of Caring. I encourage couples to make a list of specific behaviors they want the other person to do for them that reflect caring. Then they exchange lists. Both try to meet a certain agreed-upon number from the list each day.

Let me give samples of items from Bob's and Debbie's lists:

Bob	*Debbie*
I want Debbie to:	I want Bob to:
☐ Say "I love you"	☐ Call me from work
☐ Give me a back rub	☐ Help with Saturday chores
☐ Listen to me	☐ Rub my feet
☐ Fix her famous pie	☐ Tell me I'm important

☐ Go to the ball game with me   ☐ Say "I love you"
☐ Pray with me   ☐ Say "Thank you" for the meals
                                     I prepare

Bob and Debbie agreed to do at least three items a day from the lists. They were responsible to choose what they wanted to do for the other person. The contract between them rested on the fact they would complete their personal choices regardless if the other person completed theirs.

Principle of Expectations. Everyone has expectations for how the other person in a relationship needs to act. ACAs are prone to have perfectionistic expectations for their spouses. Three important ingredients are helpful in dealing with expectations. First, learn to ask for what you want. By talking with your spouse you will clarify your requests and discover which ones are too high.

Second, behind many expectations are unmet needs. For instance, a client wanted her husband to not become an elder at a church. Behind the request was the fear of being abandoned by the demands of the position. By dealing with the deeper issue, they could devise workable solutions for both.

Third, free the spouse to not meet the needs. By doing so you lower the sense of trying to control the other. What your mate does becomes a gift given to you. Besides, the truth is we cannot control each other.

Principle of Meaningful Touch. I think it is a sad commentary when I hear people joke about how a couple must be married because they do not touch. ACAs in particular need to address this issue. I believe the couple misses an important healing activity if there is not enough touch. Giving hugs and back rubs, holding hands, sitting together, kissing and touching without the motive of going to bed for sexual lovemaking creates deeper emotional and sexual bonding.

Principle of a Spiritual Life. Couples that develop a spiritual component to their marriage have a more meaningful purpose. They have a vision that extends beyond the daily routine and struggles they face.

They capture a sense of connection with a power that can energize and heal their relationship. They are able to forgive because they have been forgiven, comfort with the comfort they received, accept the other because they have been accepted and commit because they know what it feels to have someone committed to them.

I encourage couples to return to their spiritual roots and build this important area back into their lives. All the principles, techniques and recovery concepts pale when compared to the insights for living and healing God provides.

Wear Compassion

I hope you find a principle that you can apply to your situation. Don't be overwhelmed by trying to put them all into effect. Also, as you build awareness about your relationship and face what is there, remember to comfort each other and build acceptance in your relationship. Then, take some action to live differently today in your relationship. Sit down with your spouse and review this chapter. If your spouse is not open to some of the concepts, you decide what fits for your situation and put them into practice.

I want to end with a favorite Scripture of mine, Colossians 3:12-13. I'm going to expand the concepts presented with a paraphrase of what it means to me.

Clothe yourselves	Like getting dressed each day, put on the following items:
with compassion,	realize you both hurt like burn victims;
kindness,	find ways to care for each other;
humility,	neither is more important than the other but both are important;
gentleness	develop a comforting lifestyle with each other;
and patience.	and build a "one-day-at-a-time" attitude because recovery is a slow process.

Bear with each other	Realize you are in this together, so pull the plow together;
and forgive whatever grievances you may have against one another.	and after owning your pain learn to let go by forgiving, and try to keep short accounts with each other.

May you both continue to heal individually and together.

14
THE JOURNEY CONTINUES

♦ ♦ ♦

As I come to the end of this book, I feel relief, joy, a sense of accomplishment and satisfaction. But I also feel sadness and a sense of incompleteness. There are many areas I left out in our discussion. There are ideas I'm not sure I really communicated as clearly as I had wanted. It is the perfectionist within me raising its ugly head and pointing out the flaws and incomplete parts of the book. So even in writing about recovery I am faced with my own need of continued recovery work.

Key Recovery Tasks
I want to close this book with a final look at the primary areas of recovery. In chapter three I explained the AAA recovery format. This is effective because recovery work is a constant task of building *awareness,* increasing *acceptance* and taking constructive *action* steps. Since the thrust of this book is early recovery issues, let me list some of the

key tasks necessary for recovery.

Facing Our Problems. We need to develop understanding about the causes of our problems as adults. The thesis of this book is that our patterns as adults were formed when we were children. We learned to relate to ourselves and others from the teachings of our family and from the society at large.

We also need to be honest with ourselves about the patterns we discover in our lives. We've looked at patterns of emotions, thoughts and behaviors. In facing ourselves, we have to be honest about what we see, how it affects us and how it continues to perpetuate an unhealthy and dysfunctional style of living. It is true that our patterns were once essential for survival. But in the long run these patterns will only perpetuate our pain. When examining our lives, we need to confront the denial mechanisms we learned as children.

There are many strategies we could use to face our problems. These include writing, attending workshops and seminars, reading books, listening to lectures, and support groups. The key to developing awareness is to learn to face what is rather than what should be, and to use the available resources to increase an understanding about self, early home life and how that home life has affected us as adults.

Learning to Feel Again. Recovery work means developing permission to feel which is important because so much of our pain is left unhealed within us. We develop strategies to survive, but in the end these strategies create as much, if not more, pain.

Learning to feel again helps to bring the parts within us back together. As children we tended to split off what we feel, and what we think and how we behave so there is little organization between these three parts. This splitting helps us to survive as children, but as adults it only creates more pain. Learning to feel again allows healing a chance to occur and cuts down the splitting of the parts within us.

Learning to feel again is essential for grieving and healing the numerous losses that each of us has experienced. Without this grieving process these losses remain for the duration of our lives.

Taking Responsibility for Ourselves. We are not responsible for how we were raised as a child, but we are responsible for the actions we take as adults. No matter what's been done to you, only you will be able to affect the change in your life from this day forward.

For many of us our parents are not even alive. For many our parents are unavailable. Some of our parents are resistant to the idea that they did anything wrong. For them all this recovery talk does not make sense. It is hard to face the fact that we are the only ones with the power to make a change in our own lives. It is within our power to reach out to God and to other people and heal our wounds.

Eliminating Self-Hate and Building a Sense of Respect. I have presented the need for accepting and comforting ourselves as important tools for the healing journey. Without eliminating our basic self-hatred and lack of respect for ourselves, we are doomed to a life that seeks to prove that we are important in our own right. In such a case we will find the strategies we use as adults are those we used as children. Ultimately these cause more harm than good.

Healing the Inner Child. As children our hearts were wounded. A great deal of time needs to be given to the healing and the nurturing of the inner feelings. This is like taking a heart that's been broken and over a period of time of gentle nurturing and comforting putting it back together. This process allows the heart to mend, the brokenness to heal and the joy to return.

Identifying and Removing Escape Behaviors. Our misguided attempts to escape can become chronic. Escape behaviors, after establishing themselves as chronic, bring a great deal of remorse, loss of self-respect and a sense of hopelessness.

At first, these escapes gave us relief. But they ended up increasing our pain, our shame and our self-blame. To break these escape behaviors you may find it necessary to join a support group, a strong church fellowship or group therapy. You may also find it essential to remove yourself from people or situations where your escape behaviors are encouraged. This can be extremely difficult. However, in order to succeed, it is imperative that we recognize how we act and in what circumstances we act, and then make decisions that are in our best interest based upon this information.

Connecting with Someone We Can Trust. One of the most frightening things we can do is trust someone. This is a stumbling block to many in recovery. We need to trust, and yet we find that trusting is hard to do. Choose a pastor, a minister, a friend or family member who is honest with their own recovery path. Sometimes a person can be found in a support group or a meeting where the topics covered are related to our recovery issues. But we must find one person somewhere and begin building trust with him or her.

I also believe it is important to risk trusting in God. In my own recovery there were times that trusting in God was too abstract. It did not seem very real. But over time, I began to understand that God is constant. He is the same yesterday, today and forever. His desire for me and for you is that we have healing and a deeper understanding about his role in our lives. He seeks to reconcile his children to himself. He desires a relationship with us based on honesty and compassion and grace. Trusting anyone is hard and trusting someone you cannot see is even more difficult. But a part of our recovery is learning to ask for the help we need and to trust that God will provide and enable us to face our pain.

Developing a Spiritual Component to Our Journey. I stated before that the healing journey involves ourselves, others and our spiritual lives. It is not essential to have a theological degree to understand that all of us are spiritual beings. Developing a spiritual component to our journey of recovery may take the form of a church fellowship, a small group, a prayer fellowship or a men's breakfast meeting. It may be a 12-step program that emphasizes a higher power, or it may be a Christ-centered 12-step program that emphasizes a more active and

personal relationship with God. You may find it important to read the
Bible and spend time in prayer and meditation seeking to know truth
and seeking to understand your own spiritual life with God.

Learning to Ask for What We Want and Need. Most of us raised in
dysfunctional homes do not understand what we need and want. Also,
we do not know how to ask for what we want. A part of recovery is
developing the understanding of what we want and need. This helps
us fill the holes in our hearts and provide the missing pieces from our
childhood development.

But it is not enough to simply know what we need, it is equally
important to learn to ask for what we want. A part of recovery is to
learn that no one knows what we need but us. No one can meet our
needs except ourselves, so we need to ask for the things we need.

Learning to Let Go of What We Cannot Get. Most of us have the
experience of not getting what we need. It is difficult to build an
awareness of what we need, develop the courage to ask for what we
need, and then be faced with the possibility that it will not be given
to us. For most of us it takes a long time to learn to let go of what
we cannot get. When I work with couples, I often encourage them to
ask for what they want and at the same time free the other person
to never do it.

For most of us raised in dysfunctional homes controlling our environment is extremely important. If we can control our environment
then we are able to make the world go according to the way we think
it ought to go. This means I'm not going to have to face my pain, and
I'm not going to have to face conflict, and I'm not going to have to
face difficult emotions, and, in general, I will not have to do my
recovery work. In early recovery, as adult children experience the
feelings that come with not getting important needs met during childhood, a sense of courage envelops them. Then it is very common to
take a bold stand and ask for the things they did not get as children.
This is very important and vital to recovery work. However, a tough

lesson begins to be learned when life does not give what we think it ought to give. Learning to let go of what we cannot have is as much a part of recovery work as much as learning to ask for what we need.

Setting Our Recovery in Motion Daily. Each of us really only has today. The choices we make today will reflect upon tomorrow and upon next week and upon next year. If today does not produce all that we want (and it rarely does), it is important for us to bring closure to the day by acknowledging the victories and mourning the defeats. Each day given to us will have its share of heartache and its share of joy. Our recovery path through that day will become a part of the road map of our recovery journey.

I do not believe there's such a thing as a perfect day. But there are moments throughout any day when we will capture what it's like to be truly alive and what it means to be fully human. Every day we can feel joy from kindness and the healing of a gentle word.

If we were raised in a dysfunctional home our day often consists of surviving, avoiding and escaping. As we enter into our own healing journey, some of these experiences will not change immediately. But within any day of recovery there is a victory to be seen and a joy to be captured. Learning to live each day and set in motion a recovery path that focuses on the day at hand, you will slowly find that the wreckage of your past no longer burdens you and the fear of the future no longer ties you up. Without the burden of the past and the bondage of the future you have a chance to live today and experience both victory and defeat.

A Healing Story

This is Sandy's story. She has given me permission to use her life and the details about her struggles to help you in yours. I chose to maintain her anonymity by altering a few of her circumstances and by using a different name.

Sandy came to my office for counseling to deal with her depression and anxiety. Her family background was dysfunctional, full of shame and instability. As a child she felt rejected by her parents and developed a mistrust for people in authority. She was placed in a position of caring for her family's emotional needs. As a child she was overwhelmed with the responsibility of caring for the adults in her life.

As an adolescent she began to experiment with drugs and left the home. She married at a very early age and took on the lifestyle of a free-spirited hippie living in camps and cabins and wilderness places. She used many drugs and was typical of those in the hippie movement of the sixties and seventies.

She was married to a man who was a substance abuser. There was a lot of violence in their relationship. She eventually divorced him and later married a man who was alcoholic. These two marriages brought forth four children. Her own drug use became unmanageable, and her life was getting out of control.

The state children's protective services became involved in caring for her children. They removed them from Sandy's home and placed them with friends and relatives. The pain and the failure that she faced was overwhelming to her. She saw herself as a sensitive, caring and warm person with a big heart for the needs and the burdens of other people. At a very early age she came face to face with the failure of caring for the most important people in the world to her—her children. She was wounded in her heart four times as these kids were taken away one by one.

She was on the brink of suicide more than once. All hope was gone. Her faith and her belief in the fairness of life, the joy of life and the meaning of life were all stripped away. She spent time in psychiatric hospitals and numerous counseling offices. She pursued a path of various religions, yet the nagging, relentless pain would not let up.

Eventually Sandy began to find healing in her relationship with God. She began to trust in his power and in his presence in her life. And, yet, still there remained a pain that would propel her into depression. The gains that she would make in her daily path were wiped out by the depression, the hopelessness and the despair that would overtake her like a black fog.

About this time Sandy and I began a counseling relationship. Failures that she continually faced day in and day out in her recovery path were much the same as each of us has faced. She examined her family of origin and began to notice her role as caretaker for her family as well as the perfectionism, the mistrust and inadequacy, and the deep sense of shame from her family. As she continued to develop honesty with herself, we looked at the choices she made as an adult that led to her losing her children. The grief, the pain, the loss, the shame associated with those children were deep wounds in Sandy's heart.

As she continued on her recovery path she understood the choices her parents made and began to forgive them. At the same time, she realized she may never find closeness with them. When she would look at her own failures the hurt was so deep that there just did not seem, in her eyes, any way she could ever make peace with herself. She would often say, "I can understand the hurt that I brought to myself, but I don't understand how I could have brought so much pain to innocent children." Week after week Sandy rebuilt her sense of self, took responsibility for herself each day and slowly rebuilt her acceptance of herself. Her hope began to return.

She began to understand the needs within her and the escape strategies she used to try to meet those needs. She could see more clearly the ways she controlled people around her and the protection she used to keep people from her. She began to appreciate the strengths that she did have. Her sensitivity, her warm heart, her endurance, her ability to care for other people, her enthusiasm for life and her ability to take responsibility for herself all became assets on which to build a strong foundation. Over the months that passed her life became more stable and less like an emotional roller coaster. She changed her place of worship to a church that was more supportive of her and began to build a network of people that she could count on.

She was remarried to a person that she loved very much. Yet she was afraid, given her track record of relationships, that this marriage might not last either. She continued to learn what she was in charge of and could take some responsibility for and what she was not in charge of and needed to let go of. Still, all in all, the days were better, the emotions were stable, and the hope that she could live a productive life were signs of her improved condition. She began to hold on to these victories, day in and day out. But the wounds of the heart were ever so slow to heal. She would pray often for God to help in the healing of her heart and believed that it was his power and his strength that was creating the changes within her.

Still, as the birthdays of her children would come and go, the pain she experienced was very intense. All her accomplishments would pale in the face of reminders of her children. At church she would see mothers and fathers with their children, and sometimes it was all that she could do to hold back tears. There were times she avoided functions with families because her wounds would be re-opened. It seemed to me that the work of recovery we had done was good. We had made substantial changes and had given her a better life. But she was still filled with a great deal of sadness and loss. I thought that it would take a few years of continued healing before her wounds would become real tender spots in her heart. It was at this point that the therapy took a turn.

Sandy received a call from her daughter Jennifer. Jennifer wanted to reunite with Sandy and re-establish a relationship with her. Sandy was immediately thrown back into the wounds of the past. The fear of facing one of the children that she had failed crippled her. Her anxiety and her dread led Sandy to postpone meeting her daughter. The very thing that she had prayed for, that is, to be reunited with her children, was dropped in her lap, and she was terrified.

Finally, after much apprehension, she met Jennifer, and the two cried and talked and began to establish a meaningful relationship.

This produced mixed blessings for Sandy. On the one hand she was excited and happy for the newfound relationship. And on the other hand she still felt the sadness and grief and loss from the other relationships with her children. In a short time Jennifer gave birth to a child and Sandy began to experience the feelings of mothering that she had never really experienced when her children lived with her. In her new capacity as a grandmother she received a lot of healing as she nurtured and comforted her daughter and her granddaughter. There were times that Sandy stood in disbelief in her relationship with her daughter and her granddaughter. She was amazed at the restoration of the relationship.

Over the next several months her other children made contact with her. Each contact brought forth many emotions and much indecision. But with her courageous attitude she pursued re-establishing relationships with each child. Some of the relationships were closer than others, but all of them began to produce more healing and help within Sandy. Each day she was thankful for the opportunity that God had given to her in healing the brokenness with her children.

Later, in her job in a hospital, she was transferred to a position in pediatrics. One of her jobs in this new assignment was the nurturing and comforting of the children in the clinic. Each day there were moments of sadness and joy for her. Slowly, she was able to experience healing and comfort because she could demonstrate to so many children the love that she felt for them.

She was overwhelmed one day in my office as she looked back to the brokenness and the years of separation from her family. She realized how much healing had taken place and how much the relationships were being restored. She commented one day, "I fully understand what God meant when he promised to restore the years the locusts have eaten" (Joel 2:25).

While there are many stories of healing and hope I could present,

I thought it appropriate to present the story of Sandy, her broken past, her tragic adulthood and her mended present.

I believe strongly in the desire within each of us for healing. And I believe strongly that recovery work produces healing within us. Sandy and I worked hard together in counseling. Sandy herself completed some hard recovery tasks. But I believe strongly that God facilitated the healing process within her in a way we could never foresee. Given the amount of damage in the relationships with her children, she thought the best she could hope for was that they would forgive her and be able to live a life that was not forever torn apart. She did not dream that the relationships between her and her children would ever be restored. But it is for that reason I believe that recovery is a spiritual journey.

Recovery means facing what's real today, healing the past and maintaining hope in God. He truly wants each of us to experience healing and find the peace which transcends all understanding.

Comforting Others

There are many questions that remain unanswered and many ideas I've yet to present, but I pray that each of you on a healing path will find a piece of the puzzle that fits and build upon it. I desire that you will build *awareness*, develop more *acceptance* of yourself, and devise *action* strategies for healing in your life.

Let me close with one of my favorite passages. "Praise be to the God and Father of our Lord Jesus Christ, the Father of compassion and the God of all comfort, who comforts us in all our troubles, so that we can comfort those in any trouble with the comfort we ourselves have received from God" (2 Corinthians 1:3-4). Each of us will eventually touch lives that are as pained and broken as our own. As we heal and experience comfort and forgiveness within ourselves we can assist others along this healing journey.

Bibliography

Briggs, Dorothy Corkville. 1977. *Celebrate Your Self.* Garden City, N.Y.: Double-day & Co., Inc.

Brown, Stephanie. 1988. *Treating Adult Children of Alcoholics: A Developmental Perspective.* New York: John Wiley & Sons, Inc.

Byram, Alice. 1988. *Healing the Broken Places.* Colorado Springs, Colo.: Nav-Press.

Erikson, E. H. 1963. *Childhood and Society.* Second Edition. New York: W. W. Norton & Co.

Fried, John, and Fried, Linda. 1988. *Adult Children: The Secrets of Dysfunctional Families.* Deerfield Beach, Fla.: Health Communications.

Glenn, H. Stephen, and Nelson, Jane. 1987. *Raising Children for Success.* Fair Oaks, Calif.: Sunrise Press.

James, John W., and Cheny, Frank. 1988. *The Grief Recovery Handbook.* New York: Harper & Row Publications.

Kritsberz, Wayne. 1985. *The Adult Children of Alcoholics Syndrome.* Deerfield Beach, Fla.: Health Communications.

Larsen, Ernie. 1988. *Old Patterns, New Truths.* San Francisco: Calif.: Harper & Row.

Lasater, Lane. 1988. *Recovery from Compulsive Behaviors.* Deerfield Beach, Fla.: Health Communications.

Linn, Dennis, and Linn, Matthew. 1978. *Healing Life's Hurts.* New York: Paulist Press.

Middleton-Moz, Jane. 1989. *Children of Trauma.* Deerfield Beach, Fla.: Health Communications.

Middleton-Moz, Jane, and Diveneil, Lorie. 1986. *After the Tears.* Deerfield Beach, Fla.: Health Communications.

Rosellini, Gayle, and Worden, Mark. 1987. *Taming Your Turbulent Past.* Deerfield Beach, Fla.: Health Communications.

Schiff, Jacqui L., et al. 1975. *The Cathexis Reader: The Transactional Analysis Treatment of Psychosis.* New York: Harper & Row.

Seamands, David A. 1985. *Healing of Memories.* Wheaton, Ill.: Victor Books.

Seixes, Judith S., and Youcha, Geraldine. 1985. *Children of Alcoholism: A Survivor's Manual.* New York: Harper & Row.

Standacher, Carol. 1987. *Beyond Grief.* Oakland, Calif.: New Harbinger Publications, Inc.

Weinhold, Barry, and Weinhold, Janae. 1989. *Breaking Free of the Co-Dependency Trap.* Walpole, N.H.: Stillpoint Publishing.

Whitfield, Charles L. 1987. *Healing the Child Within.* Deerfield Beach, Fla.: Health Communications.

Wilson, Sandra D. 1989. "Evangelical Christian Adult Children of Alcoholics: A Preliminary Study." *Journal of Psychology and Theology,* 17, 263-273.

Woititz, Janet Beringer. 1983. *Adult Children of Alcoholics.* Deerfield Beach, Fla.: Health Communications.